A Wife's Recovery from an Affair:

The Story of a Faithful God

April Truitt

Table of Contents

A Letter to the Reader

Hello, Beautiful Reader.

You may be broken, but you are beautiful. You have a journey of recovery ahead of you. I once was where you are, asking the same questions you have. Why was my spouse unfaithful? Do I stay or leave my marriage? Will the tears ever stop? How can I forgive? You are not alone. I want to walk with you and offer hope and nuggets of truth from my journey in affair recovery.

Jesus, I ask for your presence and love to comfort this dear reader. Hold and comfort them as they begin this journey of recovery. Give them wisdom and strength to work through the heartache and loss. Fill them with hope in You and the courage to press on.

Acknowledgments

First, all glory and praise to God for His mercy and love working in my life. He is my anchor and the life in my lungs. Thank you, Jesus, for redeeming me and my marriage and never leaving me.

Kenny, by God's grace, may we continue to let Him mold and shape us into His image. I am thankful that through the faithfulness of God, we are reconciled and together. Thank you for the strengths and giftings you offer our family. Thank you for being a father who invests in his children and seeks to show them a better example. Thank you for your willingness to let our story be shared so that others can be encouraged and recognize that all of us are sinners in need of a Savior. Thank you for working with God to rewrite our story.

Jessica, thank you for the vast wisdom you shared with professional counseling. Your dedication to correctly handling the Word of God made an impact on our sessions.

Thank you to our church friends at Crossroads Church, and Kingdom Impact who invested in us.

Praying, encouraging, supporting, and walking with us through that difficult season.

Jennifer, Thank you for being my lifeline that first day. Your willingness to be open and honest with your marriage helped encourage and steady me.

Diana, thank you for your friendship and the ways you welcomed me—your words of encouragement and prayers. Your kindness and friendship gave me a "home" to rest in.

Priscylla, thank you for your mentorship, encouragement, and prayers.

Myrna, I appreciated all those gatherings in your home. Your home was a place of refuge and hospitality. Wonderful memories were made there. Your love and support during that season was so valuable.

Thank you to our family who supported us, prayed for and offered forgiveness.

Aunt Janet, you will never know the kingdom impact you made by faithfully being an example of Christ and always speaking the truth in love. I am so thankful for the treasure you are as a spiritual mentor. Thank you for speaking life and always reminding me of God's Word and His ways.

Charlee, thank you for being a safe place for me and grieving with me.

Mom and Dad thank you for respecting our process and growth. For your forgiveness, love, and support.

Melissa thank you for being a sounding board for me with any need I have shared. Thank you for praying when I have no words. For being present when I just need to know I'm not alone.

Thank you, Cherrilynn, for editing my book. Your encouragement and advice were so helpful.

Thank you to the Global Publishing team. Your communication was great and your work was prompt. I never imagined publishing would go as smoothly as it has.

Thank you to my launch team for supporting me by helping to get the book out there!

Thank you to those not mentioned by name who walked beside us in this journey with prayers, friendship, mentorship, and support. God used each and every one of you.

About the Author

April is a first-time author, wife, mother of three, speaker, blogger, and Christian singer/songwriter. She and her spouse have been married for twenty-one years. Her experience has encompassed affair recovery and restoration, Christian women's ministry, inspirational speaking, activity coordinating, and singing-songwriting.

Developing a deep relationship with Jesus as a young teen, her spiritual walk, has taken her through many challenges. An unshakable faith and trust in God were forged through the deepest pain and fear.

Through her writing and speaking events April helps discouraged women find hope and security by pointing them to the God whose presence changes everything. Sharing her experience with betrayal, rejection, and hitting rock bottom, women will hear of a God who is faithful when all else fails, enabling them to overcome overwhelming circumstances.

Do you have a speaking event you would like to book April for? Check out www.apriltruitt.com or email her at apriltruittspeaker@gmail.com

Prologue

The moon was luminous and full that September night in 2016. Relishing the solitude, I slipped out the door into the evening ocean breeze.

Were the waves glimmering with blue tonight? The remarkable bluish flare of tiny plankton, my first experience with bioluminescence, happened the night before on the shore of Duck, North Carolina. God's creation captivated me. Here, on the edge of the dark expanse of waters, I came to meet with my Creator.

There were no voices around me besides the hiss of the incoming waves. Sure, I was safe and alone; I pulled the headphones over my ears. Reaching up to the stars, I swayed to the melodies of praise, my spirit agreeing with the words of worship. Dashing into the surf, I playfully jumped and twirled, the breeze grabbing the strands of my hair in a gentle dance. God was here in this moment. He was present with me as I was with Him.

Father, I need you. Be with Kenny. Lord, I don't know where he is with You spiritually. Draw your son to You. God, there's such a distance between Kenny and me. I don't know how to fix this shallowness I feel. I want to share You with him, be on the same page together, and grow as a couple. Work in our marriage, Father. Lord, I give him to You. Do the work that needs to be done in his heart to walk faithfully with You again.

"It is Well" by Bethel Music started to play. Considering my worries, I equated the lyric's mountains being thrown into the midst of the sea to my spouse's faith struggle with God.

I didn't know that this was only the beginning of bigger mountains. I couldn't anticipate the heights that would drive me to my knees.

Faced with the darkened, watery surface stretching beyond the horizon, I leaned into God's comforting presence. If I focused on Him, it would be well with my soul.

1

A Confession

I squeezed my husband's hand. I felt romantic and giddy as I shared my hopes and dreams for this new venture. There had been an emotional distance between us for a long time, but this weekend, Kenny seemed affectionate and tuned in. I soaked up his attention as we drove toward Stafford, Virginia.

We'd spent grueling months trying to fix our home in Franklin, Virginia, to make it more marketable. I cherished the break from packing. I didn't care that a blow-up mattress awaited our tired bodies. We were together and happy.

Our new townhouse in Stafford echoed our footsteps as we waited for our furniture and belongings to arrive in several weeks. We dumped our weekend bags in the master bedroom. This "camp-out" was in anticipation of our second Tough Mudder event the next day.

We stepped outside and chatted with our new neighbors. I was excited by the connections we made and the friendliness we were met with among our neighbors. Socializing with them would be the new normal.

The following day, Kenny and I jogged in place, stretched our legs, and joined the runners, waiting for the whistle to signal it was time to cross the starting line. The shrill sound was followed by a mass of bodies surging forward onto the muddy course. Not being great runners, we jogged half the time and walked the rest between the challenges. I relied on Kenny's muscles for the obstacles that required upper body strength.

Mud caked our shoes, grit hid behind our ears, and we were soaked from head to toe. We stood in front of the finisher's selfie wall. I handed our phone to a fellow mud runner, jumped piggyback on Kenny, and smiled for a photo. I felt cherished, and the run added playfulness to our relationship.

However, that was the last time my world would feel secure for a long time.

After returning home to Franklin on Sunday, we continued the packing process. Tuesday, we headed into our routine marriage counseling session.

During the last year, Kenny went through an intense time of counseling and healing from sexual abuse in his past. We had also been working with our counselor, Jessica, on marriage communication and conflict resolution.

Typically, we discussed concerns or things we felt needed to be worked on while driving to our session.

I turned toward Kenny. "I haven't thought much about what we'll discuss today. I feel like we've been doing well."

As we exited the car, his face was neutral, quiet, and reserved. Internally, I felt good about our move coming up and was encouraged by the past year of counseling we had been through. I felt we had learned the tools for better communication and wanted to suggest to her today that we discontinue our sessions.

Jessica's office was small but cozy, with warm lighting, a sofa, and homeopathy décor on the walls. We sat in our usual places as she pulled a chair opposite us. Something about the tension in the air made my senses kick in.

Jessica locked eyes with me. "Kenny had this session set up, and we have extra time to talk things out if needed."

My spirit went on the defensive. I was fully aware and present then, and every sense was heightened. Time slowed I waited, bracing for something I knew I could feel was coming. Beside me, Kenny was rubbing his hands together, his eyes downcast. He lifted his head and turned to me, "I had an affair with Taylor."

The name shocked me. I heard the words "I had an affair" and filled in the blank myself. But the name was not the same. The girl I had filled the blank with was more of an acquaintance he had admitted to being attracted to.

Jessica's words broke into my shock. "Did you know this? Or expect this?"

"No, not Taylor." It would have been more bearable if it had been someone else, but Taylor? Taylor was my weak spot, the one I tried the hardest to control when he was around her. I loved her, and our families had been on vacation together. We lived across the states from each other but made the most of the time we had when we were together.

Though I loved her, I knew she was a guy magnet. I was her shadow growing up. Guys ate out of her hand because of her fun and confident personality. Her body was model-worthy, and her countenance oozed sexy. Growing up, I didn't put effort into that sort of thing, but as a married woman, whenever she was around, I put extra effort into my clothing and makeup simply because I wanted to hold my own somehow next to her. I didn't want her to outshine me.

I dropped extra weight and had my hair cut in a short, sexy Victoria Beckham style. Our husbands commented on how much we looked similar, almost like sisters.

As we sat on the couch in Jessica's office, I felt strangely detached from so much of the conversation. It was like I was talking about someone else, not myself, not our marriage. My emotions of shock, anger, hurt, sympathy, hate, love, sickness, and numbness were too much to process.

I had questions,

"When did this start?"

"How long did it last?"

"It started in October when she came to see us. Then, I flew out to see her for three days during the week of Christmas." My husband confessed.

How was I to suspect? With his shift work schedule, it was not uncommon for him to be gone for two to three days, especially if he got overtime at his fire station. With this new information, I was angry about Christmas, remembering how long he had been gone that week and how he seemed busy and distracted. It had been such a busy week for me and the kids. Now, I understood his emotional distance.

More thoughts and questions ran through my head.

What if something happened to us during that time? I did all the cleaning and prepping that week to host our extended family's Christmas celebration while he cheated on me with her.

I couldn't think of anything more to ask. I wanted to go home to think and process. "April, I want to be with you. I will do whatever it takes to keep you if you choose to stay with me," Kenny petitioned.

"We would like you to give the marriage six months before deciding if you want to leave and divorce," Jessica requested.

I decided to think about it. Our session ended earlier than usual.

We walked to the car, and he opened the door for me. I texted my best friend Melissa before he could get in and shut his door.

Pray hard for me right now -April

Melissa and I shared a deep friendship for over 20 years.

"If you don't want to teach your Group Fight class tonight, you shouldn't," he said after starting the engine.

I became certified and taught at our local YMCA.

"No, I'm going to teach. I think it will be good for me."

Kicking, and boxing, some frustrations out sounded appealing.

He gripped tighter to the steering wheel, "Do you think you want to contact Jennifer?"

"Yes, I will see if she can meet with me sometime this week."

Jennifer was a friend from our church. She and her husband had overcome an affair four years earlier. God gave her the grace to forgive her spouse, and their marriage was healed and restored. At that moment, she was the only local person I knew who had gone through betrayal and knew exactly how I felt.

The car radio played. I was quiet and reflective. In my peripheral, I noticed his face twitching with pain and worry; in agony, he silently held his emotions in. He used significant amounts of self-control to give me space and allow me to react and process as needed. He did not want to lose me.

Later he told me he struggled against God's voice for months, pressing him to tell me the truth. It was no surprise he feared telling me, as I said multiple times, that infidelity would be intolerable for me. He knew if he ever cheated on me, I would walk out the door and not look back.

In the silence, I craved comfort from God. I pulled index cards from my purse. These were verses that I had written to claim God's promises after doing Beth Moore's "Breaking Free" workbook. I read the verses out loud, claiming the promises, as my spirit needed God's strength. In this moment of brokenness and pain, when the world I had just known was turned upside down, I would say what I knew was true; what I knew was trustworthy.

Kenny smiled, also soaking in the promises of God.

After returning home, I shoved exercise gear into my gym bag and left early for the YMCA. I needed to get away from him so I could think. I texted Jennifer, our friend from church, and asked if she could meet me after my fight class to talk. She responded right away. Knowing I would have someone to talk to within the next few hours who could sympathize and advise me was comforting.

The ball fields behind the YMCA were my escape. I had to walk and release this torrent of feelings. I called Melissa, and we talked as I made circles around the grassy wooded areas behind the facility. She was the first person I confided in. I'd been a support to her during her struggles as well. She was my sounding board. She knew me well. Though states and time may have separated us, each conversation was picked back up with the intimacy and love we shared from a "bosom friend" relationship that I compared to the character Anne of Green Gable's relationship with Diana. We just picked up where we left off. Her prayers and support got me through many times. Melissa didn't know what to say and was shocked, but I knew she was standing with me and praying for us, which was the comfort I needed.

I taught my Group Fight class, which required my focus and attention. What a blessed relief from the turbulence of the morning.

An hour later, I pulled into a parking space at the local golf club. Relief flooded me as Jennifer's head poked out of her car. Her petite frame slid through the door. This friendly face was my only hope for the answers I was dying to get. We made strides on the golf course trails for two hours in the golden hues of the late afternoon.

Only a few weeks prior, my husband and I were guests at Jen's home. She and I talked indoors about food, cats, and life while Kenny was outside with her husband, Philip, warning him of the storm to come and my upcoming need for support from Jennifer. She'd known this day would come and was ready to support me. I rambled and spewed. Sharing facts and asking questions. Calm, reflective, and sweet in spirit, her tranquil presence provided me with the space and freedom to open up, and she candidly shared their story.

Jennifer gave me a crucial treasure from that conversation. She asked God to give her a word after she found out about her husband's affair. God told her to fight for her marriage. And she did.

"April, you need a word. Ask God to give you one. Then you will know what to do. You will be at peace to move forward."

"How long did you wait to renew sexual intimacy?" I asked.

She said because she felt God wanted her to fight and she had decided to stay, they didn't wait long to renew sexual intimacy. She did say there were moments she would have to stop them because it might be too emotionally painful, but she sought to continue to connect and heal with him in the aftermath.

The last glow of the setting sun was fading on our outdoor talk, and I still had lots to sift through as I hugged her and got back in my car.

I don't want to go back and face him. I'm still not ready to go home. I parked the car alongside a nearby city park and journaled from the car's comfort.

Father, please give me a scripture verse. I need a word from you.

I tapped my phone, and the screen lit up with the verse of the day from my Bible app.

Matthew 5:14-16 (Message Version): "Here's another way to put it: You're here to be light, bringing out the God-colors in the world. God is not a secret to be kept. We're going public with this, as public as a city on a hill. If I make you light-bearers, you don't think I'm going to hide you under a bucket, do you? I'm putting you on a light stand. Now that I've put you there on a hilltop, on a light stand-shine! Keep open house; be generous with your lives. By opening up to others, you'll prompt people to open up with God, this generous Father in Heaven."

My journal entry.

June 13th, 2017: *My mind is tired. Kenny and I went to counseling this afternoon. He confessed to having an affair with (Taylor). It felt like a dream. It still does. I feel oddly disconnected from it. I feel flashes of anger, pain, sympathy, hate, love, sickness, numbness...He is repentant...I have much to process. My worst nightmare happened. I'm now a woman betrayed and cheated on. I feel broken. Sex has always been so special for me. I have saved and shared only the most intimate parts of myself with him.......*

Now I wonder what it was like for him; how much better was she than me? He says he still loves me and loved me then, but why did he do it? How do I trust him again? And when everything rides on his relationship with Jesus, all it would take is for him to walk away again and fall. Is his faith going to be real? Will he keep walking with God, or will we go through this again?

I'm writing this from the car in the park. I don't want to go home and face him. He is afraid I will hurt myself or leave him. I felt loving and close to him this weekend... I felt loved, like I hadn't felt from him in a long time.

Jesus, give me a word. Confirm over and over to me what you want and how you want me to live. I cannot do this without You. Holy Spirit, take away my hate and give me love; take away my pride and give me humility. Take away my fears and give me trust in You.

Take away the lies and fill my mind with your truth. I need you like never before, Jesus. Meet with me! Don't let Satan destroy me, Kenny, or our marriage. In Your light, we see light.

I slipped into our kitchen through the back door. It was quiet. I passed by the living room, and the only light was from embers in the fireplace. Kenny burned an inspirational journal Taylor gave him. As crazy as it was, God used her to launch a spiritual revival in him. They bonded over their shared similar backgrounds of childhood sexual abuse. During the trip, an affair began between Kenny and her. I had told her about his resistance to spiritual things, and she told me that she wanted to encourage him to move towards God.

She lost her virginity to an older male babysitter. She acted out in sexual ways and had many sexual partners.

Kenny was about four years old when he was first sexually abused by a slightly older girl.

Unknown to his parents, the next-door neighbor entrapped him in habitual sin for several years; guilt carried on for years even after the abuse ceased.

He buried his emotions even deeper and struggled, knowing he broke God's law, and wondered if God could forgive him for falling into the thoughts and habits over and over.

Kenny grew up in a Christian home and lived a Christian life. He prayed for salvation as a young boy. But after we married, he shifted and preferred more secular things. He seemed distracted at church, and it looked like he was going through the motions.

I felt uncomfortable bringing up spiritual things with him. He listened when I brought up my relationship with God but wouldn't comment. I felt like I was losing him and that the spiritual part of our marriage was dead.

Through the years, I had been Kenny's idol, and he poured his love and affection upon me. He wanted me to be his savior. He desired a romantic, Hollywood-style, passionate love relationship with me, desiring my adoration in return.

The problem is that he expected his idol to fulfill him. Unfortunately, I was inherently selfish, emotionally detached, and prideful.

Through every fight, I stonewalled him until he was the first to seek restoration. I could not humbly admit fault. I always tried to excuse myself somehow or shrug off my part. As a peacemaker by heart, he was the glue that kept us together in many ways, but over time, my stubborn ways and selfishness wore him down.

His frustrations over work, finances, and our marriage made him angry. Not just angry at life but angry at God. I didn't realize how far gone he had become, but he said he had gotten to the point where he cursed God and decided he would show the Almighty a thing or two. If the unhappiness he experienced in these things were how God rewarded his efforts, he would work harder and do as he pleased. If God didn't look out for him, he would do life on his terms.

Fearing the security of our marriage and his lack of spiritual interest, I picked up the book The Power of a Praying Wife and started using it. I prayed for his faith. I prayed for his temptations. I prayed for his mind, heart, reputation, future, health, trials, and spiritual revival. I prayed boldly,

"Jesus, he is your son. Call him back to you. Don't let him walk away. Jesus, I claim he is your child and ask you to return him to you. Make him a man after your own heart! Draw him to you."

I fervently prayed these kinds of prayers for him. I also prayed against sexual temptation.

One of my greatest fears for our marriage was infidelity. I specifically prayed he wouldn't ever fall.

I also specifically asked God never to let that happen to my marriage. There was a feeling of being let down, that God didn't hear me and didn't choose to spare me from taking what I most treasured. He may have allowed me to go through it, but there was no doubt God never abandoned me.

At times, Kenny tried to beat his thought patterns and sin habits. He also prayed for relief from his bondage. Each time Kenny resolved to overcome sin, he would be met with failure, discouraging him and making him feel further from God. He had convinced himself he was messed up and a son of hell. He thought he must not be one of those predestined and chosen by God; that's where Taylor stepped in.

Working through the "Breaking Free" study at the time of her visit, she later sent him a section about being a rebellious child of God. God used that to grab ahold of his heart. For the first time in a long road of hopelessness, he saw that maybe, just maybe, he was a child of God. He was living in rebellion, and God was calling his prodigal back to him.

We ordered the "Breaking Free" workbooks through Taylor's prompt and started working through them together.

Your Journey, Your Story

You just found out your spouse has been unfaithful. This may have come through a confession or by discovering this betrayal yourself. On the day of discovery, it will feel like the rug was pulled out from under you. Your image of the marriage has come crumbling down to a reality you do not recognize. It feels overwhelming. Life after the disclosure of the affair is forever changed.

You have a journey ahead of you—a journey you did not volunteer for. The last thing you want to do is pull on your hiking boots and approach this mountain. Shock is a very real experience in these first days. You may struggle with denial, want to crawl into a hole, or bury your head in the sand. I tried to pretend this wasn't my life—not my marriage—but it was.

Give yourself grace. It will take time to process. I encourage you to find a verse to hold onto during this time. A verse that reminds you of an attribute of God. What does God promise to be for you? For me, it was His presence. My greatest comfort was knowing He was with me and would never leave me.

Lamentations 3:28-33

(The Message)

28-30 "When life is heavy and hard to take,

go off by yourself. Enter the silence.

Bow in prayer. Don't ask questions:

Wait for hope to appear.

Don't run from trouble. Take it full-face.

The "worst" is never the worst.

31-33 Why? Because the Master won't ever

walk out and fail to return."

Questions to Consider:

Did my spouse confess, or was he caught?

Is my spouse repentant?

What emotions am I feeling?

What scripture truth can I cling to right now?

Kenny & April at the Tough Mudder

2

Digesting

The rings slid easily off my left hand. Kenny sat on the edge of our bed as I placed the wedding bands in an envelope and plopped them into our lockbox. With a doleful face, he grieved but restrained himself from interfering with my process. It had been a rough first week.

Swinging into a Christian bookstore later, I perused the jewelry display case, seeking a True Love Waits ring. I'd worn one before, through my teen years. That was to symbolize my promise to remain a virgin until I was married, a promise I kept until our wedding day. It also symbolized the marriage vow commitment I'd made between Jesus and me.

At seventeen, I got a magazine called "Brio" for teen girls. It encouraged them to commit to a love-relationship marriage vow to Jesus.

So, on a rainy Valentine's Day in 2001, I stepped out onto the gravel of my parent's long country driveway. I had twisted my long blonde hair and pinned it with pearl barrettes. A pearl necklace encircled my throat, and I had a white cardigan wrapped around me to keep out the wet, rainy cold.

Clutching the words of the vow under my arm, I walked, holding an umbrella. Giddy, as a bride, I was starry-eyed and excited about this special private event between my First Love and me. After saying my vows to Jesus, I framed the words and hung the marriage certificate in my room.

I was so in love with Jesus. The hours I spent walking in prayer created a deep bond with the Lord. My True Love Waits ring had a lot of meaning to me. Since I couldn't bear to wear my wedding ring, the only person I wanted to be bound to after Kenny's affair was Jesus.

A haze of gloom enveloped me when Kenny went to work that week. He feared my emotional state and spending too much time alone. I'd told a few friends, but feeling shame, I tried to bottle it up inside. None of our family knew except for Kenny's sister, who had watched the children for our counseling session.

I texted my other sister-in-law, Charlee, and asked if I could see her.

She stepped aside to let us in. I smiled brittlely. My kids were excited to see their cousins. I waited patiently and tight-lipped while she messed with the remote to turn on some cartoons for them. We quietly walked down the hallway to her room and sat cross-legged on the bed.

She listened, cried, prayed for, and comforted me. She postponed her other commitments for the day to provide me with solace. I was incredibly grateful to have her during those initial days.

She also offered to support me that weekend with a Fight class demo the YMCA was doing on Saturday.

Carrie was another person I knew whose marriage had experienced infidelity. Without telling her why I wanted to meet with her, I arranged for dinner at a local restaurant.

Wanting privacy, I scanned the tables and booths. Was anyone here who knew me? There's a booth by the window. I think the coast is clear. The menu shook as I half-heartedly looked at its offerings.

Carrie smiled and squeezed into the seat across from me. "Well, isn't this a surprise! It's good to see you." After scanning the menu, she glanced up, inquiring. Taking a deep breath, I laid out the details.

"Have you had sex since then? Have you contacted a lawyer? Have you documented the events and the confession? Are you sure it's just one girl? Maybe there were more. Have you told your parents?"

My head was spinning, and fear was creeping into the pit of my stomach.

Carrie's husband never repented and ended up marrying the other woman. She had endured custody battles, numerous deceptions, and a broken heart.

"April, why haven't you told your parents?" she gently implored.

"I don't know. Shouldn't we handle this privately? Ourselves?" I faltered.

"April, you are cut and bleeding out. You need your mom. Remember, sin hides in the darkness."

That struck me. Sin hides in the darkness.

If we tried to cover this up, where would our accountability be? What if Carrie is right? What if he acts all nice and repentant now but ends up stabbing me in the back and trying to take the children? Or what if he gets the better of me if I don't document things or get legal backup now?

I left the restaurant on a mission. I was headed straight to my parent's house.

"Mom, are you guys home tonight?" I heard Dad's playful comment in the background, "I don't know, depends!"

"Yes, we'll be here." Mom said.

Dad didn't sense my urgency. Mom knew something was off. I hung up, content that my burden would finally be resting with people I trusted deeply.

My parents listened and asked questions. Dad sat deep in thought I could sense his protective gears kicking in. He highly valued trustworthiness. He willingly trusted, but once betrayed, he required trust to be earned.

Dad's outer façade was solemn, but inner anger was awakened. He didn't trust himself to be around Kenny without causing physical harm.

I decided to stay the night with my parents. Kenny was on a 48-hour shift at work, and the kids were with a friend.

After talking to Carrie and receiving the support of my parents, I shifted from a passive victim mindset to that of a judge and accuser.

My cell rang. Kenny. I told him I was with my parents and that I had told them. He was ok with that.

"I also want you to tell your parents. I think they need to know. We need accountability and support. Sin hides in the darkness." I said.

"Ok, I will do that." He complied.

I paced the floor in the spare bedroom, gripping the phone.

"Have there been more women?"

"No. Only Taylor."

"I don't believe you; you've been with more women! You don't want to tell me. Tell me now!" I spat.

"No! April, I swear there haven't been any other women. I'll prove it to you. I'll show you anything you want," he strained with emotion.

"You're lying!" I pressed harder.

"I'm the one who confessed! I told you everything. Why would I hide this when I took the risk to tell you? If I told you, I'd have to be transparent and tell you everything. What do I have to gain from hiding now?"

"I don't believe you. There have been more, and I'm done!"

"April, please. Please, I'm telling you the truth!" His voice cracked, "I'm coming there now. I'm going to leave work."

"No, I don't want you to come."

"Baby, please let me talk to you face to face; let's talk this out. I'll tell you anything you want to know. Babe, I'm sorry. I have to go. I got an EMS call," The call ended.

I could hear the panic and emotion in his voice. He felt like he was losing me, and it terrified him. He was willing to do anything to help me see he was serious about restoring what he'd broken.

It was late, so I went to bed. He finished the emergency call and told his chief he needed to go home. While I slept, he drove to my parent's house.

I woke at six a.m. and checked my cell. He was waiting outside. I threw on clothes and brushed my hair before heading out the door.

He stood there disheveled, eyes puffy and bloodshot. I sat in the car; he crawled in beside me. Even as miserable as I made him feel, he just wanted to be near me.

Dad walked outside, stiffly making his way to the shed, avoiding us. He didn't call a greeting or speak to us. Trying to give me space, he kept his distance from Kenny, his stony silence confirming the inner wrestling.

    I express my faith and emotions through music. It was no different now. I sat at the piano, letting my fingers wander over the keys to release my melancholy emotions. For months, I had been playing a melodic tune that I loved but had no words for. Now, the words came.

Your faithful love reaches me

It's higher than the mountains

deeper than the sea

I will rest in the shadow of your wings

Your banner over me is love

You're still God, and I will sing

You're still God, my everything

You're still God, and I will sing

Of your faithfulness, Your faithfulness to me

I sang with passion. My world was turned upside down; my only comfort was that God still sat on His throne. He was still in control no matter what, and because He had always been faithful, I could trust in Him and had a reason to sing.

Later that week, we met with our assistant pastor, Denise, and she prayed over us. Kenny had another brother in Christ from our church who also struggled with infidelity and encouraged and supported Kenny and me. He was there that day, too, and joined us in prayer. Standing in the little church office gathered in a circle, Denise stopped for a moment to open her eyes and face me. Spreading her hands outward, "April, I just feel God's love over you right now, and it is like a banner of love that He is spreading over you." I warmed with this thought, picturing God's banner of love over me. Those words inspired the lyrics of the song I had written.

With the weekend approaching, I still felt torn about what to do. Should I stay? Should I leave? Didn't I technically have a Biblical out now? I'd been unhappy for a while; maybe I could leave without guilt. But I also wanted to do what God wanted.

I certainly hadn't been a saint in our marriage either. I'd been selfish and, for years, had hidden from emotional intimacy with him. I felt pressed to make a decision.

Posting a prayer request on our church's prayer wall on Facebook, I asked the women to pray hard for me to hear from God on Sunday. I didn't give details; I just needed to hear a word from God and need Him to meet me.

Sunday morning, my oldest son was sick with an upset stomach. We didn't tell the children what was going on, but they had seen me withdrawn and crying all week. My oldest, especially, was in tune, and his emotions affected him physically. I told them Daddy had hurt my feelings, and I was having a hard time healing from it, even though Daddy said he was sorry. My heart was broken, and it would take time to heal.

I was running late to church, and the worship team was already playing. I was disappointed that my favorite spot, the front row, was already full. We shuffled into the second row.

Swaying to the music, Ms. Linda, a woman full of passion for Jesus, turned around. A smile lit her face. Jubilant, pointing right at me, "There's the Mountain Mover."

I was dumbfounded. *I don't feel like a mountain mover.*

She had no idea what I was going through.

I stood with my arms lifted, singing, but I felt restless. My spirit wanted to be as close to the altar as possible. Climbing over the row of chairs, I prostrated myself on the floor. Tresses of hair fell like a curtain, covering my face.

Hands upturned in plea, "I'm here, God. Your servant is here. Meet with me. Please speak to me. What do You want, God? I'll do what you want. Speak to me." Tears washed down my cheeks.

Others came and knelt at the altar, too. Ms. Linda gently laid a hand on my back and prayed over me. As the music swelled and inspired, I wept freely. More gathered around the altar, praying.

One of the few who knew, Pastor Matt, approached my kneeling form, declaring life and victory. God has won. Speaking life and power over me and our situation, he prayed fervently. The praise continued. I felt like I'd been at the front for a long time. Hurting so badly, I didn't care; torn up with emotion, Kenny was drawn to come up near me with our oldest son.

Tears were spilling over my eldest's cheeks. *I'm a failure.* Remorsefully turning to him on the floor beside me, I confessed,

"I'm sorry I haven't been a better mom to you."

He replied, "No, you've been the best mom in the world." He collapsed in my arms, crying and hugging me tight. Cradling him, I kissed his forehead. As the music ended, we made our way back to our seats.

My son sat between us, holding onto my hand. He pulled my hand and Kenny's together. We exchanged glances. My eldest sensed the tension. He knew our marriage was in danger. His security was crumbling. Our little peacemaker wanted us together.

Pastor Matt preached that morning in Isaiah 43. He pointed out that God said not to dwell on the past.

"Behold, I am doing a new thing; now it springs forth, do you not perceive it? I will make a way in the wilderness and rivers in the desert."

Isaiah 43:19 (English Standard Version)

God was making something new. That became a verse we clung to. That passage also spoke about God making a way when there is no way. For the past several months, God had been working on Kenny, and during times of worship, God had nudged him to tell me about the affair. Kenny said that each time

God spoke to him, he would say, "No, if I tell her, she will leave me."

God's answer to Kenny's heart was I will make a way. Am I not enough for her?

After the service, we barely got home, and I told Ken I wanted to go somewhere to journal. There were so many things God had spoken to me and ways He had shown up during the service, and I wanted to document and savor each one.

I drove to my favorite walking spot, parked, and pulled out my journal.

A familiar ching. Opening my cell, I saw a Facebook message.

I didn't know her personally. This older woman from our church was someone I'd never met face-to-face.

Hello, April. I saw your (Facebook) post, and so I prayed about it, and I wanted to share this with you.

You are going through this dark tunnel, but you are not alone. The Heavenly Host of God's Angels are walking in front and all around you to the light at the end of the tunnel. You feel as though you are going ever so slow, but you are moving rather quickly (God's timing!)

The trip has been feeling like a wilderness and lonely. There is a void in your spirit that can't seem to be filled. So, hold on for the exciting time to come. God has been molding you in preparation for a new spiritual level, one you have never experienced before.

Keep strong in seeking His face, and when this is over or when you come out of the tunnel- you will have a stronger faith and stronger spirit within you. Even though you feel weary and about to faint for longing for this void to be filled, stay in the Word, and it will be so amazing to see what God has in store for you.

You have a strong desire to see God work in your life and your family's and your time with God and your faithfulness will be rewarded and restored many times over.

Please keep me updated on the blessings that are coming your way. I will continue to be praying for you in this exciting time to come. I have no idea what you have been going through, but I do know that you have a strong faith, and you want to have even more of it.

God Bless and have a great day. I wanted to tell this to you in person, but my body is very tired, and I had to rest. Hope to see you next Sunday and I go to the 9 am service.

I sat astounded. The message explained exactly how I felt. I didn't know how much God would grow me and take me to a deeper spiritual level. But my heart was gaping open with a God-sized hole only He could fill, and I was desperately longing for more of Him.

Week two rolled around for our next counseling session; I'd started formulating more questions and making a list of things I wanted to discuss. Riding shotgun, our commute to the session was slow due to traffic on I-64. Weary of the highway crawl, I asked how Kenny and Taylor had communicated.

After her visit, I checked his phone a handful of times. Although I was uncomfortable knowing there was communication between them, the threads of conversation I saw by text and Facebook Messenger weren't particularly alarming. He explained that they used an app to keep their intimate conversations private.

She initiated the affair during a visit in the fall of 2016. Enticingly, she asked if he'd be interested in a "side dish."

Several mornings during her stay, she had already been up and about before I'd awoken. One morning, she'd taken my car into town. She had met him in a parking lot after he had gotten off duty before coming home. I thought she'd gone to Starbucks or shopping.

I also remember taking her back to the airport to return home to the West Coast. Pulling up to the sidewalk drop-off, we got out to unload her bags. Hugging her goodbye, I watched Kenny help carry her bags and follow her inside until she got to her terminal. I stayed with the car in the unloading lane.

Opening a book, I waited for his return. Shouldn't be too long. I continued reading. Fifteen minutes went by, then maybe twenty. I felt fidgety. *Is he sick? Or in the bathroom?* I texted him. **Are you ok?** No response. Another small, subtle thought rose in my spirit. A thought I pushed away. *What if he's kissing her goodbye?*

In hindsight, my spirit sensed things my brain was not accepting. I did not suspect anything the morning she took my car. But one day during her stay, I forgot my son's tutoring lesson and, at the last minute, left Taylor at home. I knew Kenny would be in and out of the house that day.

Going out the door, I pointed at her and said, "Don't make a move on my man, or I'll kill you!"

"What?!" In a high-pitched squeal.

Knowing her background with men made me feel uncomfortable with them being alone together, but I didn't honestly believe she would do that. At that moment, however, insecurity was speaking, and I was throwing that statement out as a half-hearted joke.

On my way back from my son's lesson, Kenny texted me asking if I'd stop to get something at the store before coming home. I was feeling uneasy about them being there together, so I didn't respond to the text but came straight home unannounced.

As soon as I entered the house, something felt off. The living room was empty; she was in her guest room with the door closed, and he was in our master bathroom with the door closed. The atmosphere in the house was strange.

Those subtle questions rose again. *Did something happen here? Did they hear the car in the driveway? Did it break up whatever was going on?* It seemed very out of place for both to be in separate rooms, with the doors closed like they were hiding.

At this time, Kenny said nothing sexual had happened, but they had been in deep conversation before I pulled in. He felt uncomfortable for me to come in on that intimate conversation, so they separated before I entered.

A sexual encounter did occur during that visit and at Christmastime when he flew out to see her. They had spent a few days together while her husband was at work and her kids at school.

After he confessed at the counseling session, I was told that they tried to end the relationship sometime in January 2017, stopping communication or at least deciding they would not continue.

Now, traffic had become a crawl.

"Did you talk any more with her after January?"

"Yes. In the spring, I told her I felt like we should confess and come clean. She threatened to leave Jimmy and started talking about self-harm.

I bought plane tickets in March and told myself I would go and make things right. I wanted to calm her down and talk her out of leaving Jimmy. But as I headed to the airport, I started thinking about her, looking forward to seeing her again."

Thankfully, the Holy Spirit convicted his heart, and at the time, Kenny listened. Realizing he missed her, he turned the car around and returned home, knowing he'd fall back into the affair.

This was new information. I had just come to grips thinking the affair had ended in January, nearly separating at least five months from the confession. But now it felt like he had lied to me.

He hadn't attempted to conceal this information, but by talking things out, I now held new facts. My timeline of feeling "safe" with the distance of five months became smaller. Not only had he lied to me during that time, saying he was working overtime when he'd left for the airport, but he then came home saying he felt sick after he chose not to fly out to the West Coast.

The knowledge that he still had feelings for her at that time and that he came so close to almost reigniting this sexual relationship again in March filled me with fury.

I sat quietly, digesting this information. Intense emotion was building up inside me, preparing to explode.

I felt irrational. I saw only two options: fight or flight. I had to get out of the car.

In the middle of stopped traffic, I turned to the window. About seventy yards away, the neighborhood in the distance beckoned me to flee.

I saw myself sprinting through the grass to reach the fence, climb over it, and run through the yards beyond. But I had no idea what I'd do after that. It seemed senseless.

The power of anger was all-consuming. Fury won out.

I balled my fists and slammed them as hard as I could on the dashboard. I hit it blow after blow, screaming in an animalistic way, and then I turned towards him and punched his arm. He did not attempt to stop me but looked at me with sad eyes.

After a minute, I pulled my arms close to my chest, breathing heavily, trying to calm down. We hardly spoke the rest of the way. I was still angry when we arrived.

"I would like to stand if you don't mind," I told Jessica.

Her eyes darted over to assess our dysfunctional entrance. "That is fine; whatever is comfortable for you," she said.

"Ya, we talked some more in the car on the way here, and I'm just really upset right now."

I stood and talked for about fifteen to twenty minutes before I could calm down enough to sit for the rest of the time. They asked me if I would commit to working on the marriage for six months before deciding to divorce or leave the marriage.

We used affair recovery workbooks in our sessions. The materials were from the "Torn Asunder" affair recovery program by Dave Carder. I agreed to work through the workbook with him.

Feeling despondent that night, I crawled into bed around dinner time and pulled the sheet over my head. I wanted a place to hide. Emotionally drained, I pulled a Bible under the sheet tent I created.

Pastor Matt's sermon had been in Isaiah, so I started reading the chapters around the one he'd preached on. Crying, I asked God to help me.

Scanning the page with blurry vision, my heart quickened.

"See, I will make you into a sharp threshing board, new, with many teeth. You will thresh mountains and pulverize them and make hills into chaff. You will winnow them, and a wind will carry them away; a gale will scatter them. But you will rejoice in the Lord; you will boast in the Holy One of Israel." Isaiah 41:15-16 (Holman Christian Standard Bible)

The script leaped off the page and into my heart. In the midst of my overwhelming despair and deep-seated hopelessness, these words filled me with a sense of profound connection. It was as if God had personally intervened, delivering a direct and powerful response through these words.

There was that word again. *Mountains.*

On the beach in Duck, NC, a year before, I'd prayed over my spouse's lacking faith comparing it to mountains. A week before the confession, the song

"Still" by Hillary Scott mentioned God moving mountains. A few days before, Ms. Linda called me a Mountain Mover.

The word mountains became a symbol. It symbolized this overwhelming and scary hurdle, but I was reminded through countless Christian songs and scriptures that God would show me how to get over that mountain.

The scripture used the word pulverize. Well, if I was to have victory over the mountain, then I needed some training, and I couldn't think of a better place to train than the mountains themselves.

I packed my bags and left for Tennessee to stay with my best friend Melissa for a few days.

Your Journey, Your Story

"For jealousy arouses a husband's fury, and he will show no mercy when he takes revenge." Proverbs 6:34 (NIV)

Though this verse speaks above of the husband with reasons for jealousy, it can equally apply to the wife's feelings. Something valuable has been taken from you. Your jealous anger shows that you rightly perceive the injustice of the broken marriage vow.

For a Christian marriage, fidelity is a requirement. It is appropriate to feel anger, which you need to work through in the healing process. We need to express anger appropriately. Murder is not an option, so how do we healthily handle our anger? These are some things that were helpful to me:

Kickboxing, punching bag, walking outdoors in fresh air, jogging, talking to a trusted friend, beating a baseball bat against a mattress, playing the drums, journaling, screaming.

In my experience, anger comes in waves. The hardest times I had controlling it were in closed spaces. Get space if you are with your spouse and the rage is building. Walk away if needed to cool down.

One night, I felt so tempted to punch my spouse that I pulled on some shoes and left for a power run. I ran until the fury wore down.

Don't be afraid to tell God how you feel. God understands the feeling of betrayal and anger. Judas betrayed Jesus. God was rejected by his people and witnessed their unfaithfulness to Him.

"Therefore, go and give this message to Israel. This is what the LORD says: "O Israel, my faithless people, come home to me again, for I am merciful. I will not be angry with you forever."

Jeremiah 3:12 (New Living Translation)

Was God angry with Israel's unfaithfulness? Yes, and at times, that anger was intense. But there is hope. He was not angry forever. Anger will come, but it is only a season.

Questions to Consider:

What is a helpful way for you to express anger?

Have you ever thought before of God's experience with unfaithfulness?

3

Climbing Mountains

Beautiful Tennessee. My friend's house sat on a hill overlooking a lake with a mountain range in the distance. We spent some time together, but I left for day trips to think and pray. Her home was a refuge while I tried to figure out what to do.

I asked her where the good hiking areas were. She told me that Frozen Head State Park had trails that led to two different waterfalls. That sounded exciting, so I packed a backpack with snacks, mace, a journal, and a Bible to explore the park. I was excited to hike independently but also nervous, as directions and reading maps were not my strength. I didn't want to go on complicated trails where I might get turned around. Also, besides having mace with me, I had no other means of self-defense from people, let alone bears. I went into the park office to ask about the trails, get familiarized with where I was going, and take the map with me.

With little rain, neither of the waterfalls was rushing by any means, but they were beautiful, nonetheless. The first waterfall on the trail was more expansive, with a short drop. There was a clear pool it cascaded into below. Few people were on the trails, but more stopped to see these falls because they were not far from the trailhead and off the main path.

I moved on from there because I wanted to find a more secluded place to settle into for journaling. As I hiked the trail to the other waterfall further ahead, Steven Curtis Chapman's lyrics from the song "Magnificent Obsession" came to me. I started singing, remembering the lyrics only as I sang. I hadn't thought about it or heard the song in a long time.

What were the depths I was about to go through? I was about to experience God's mercy and grace in a new way. My lifelong dream of having a loyal husband was crushed.

I took great pride that we only had intercourse with each other. Though Kenny had been abused in the past, intercourse was not part of it. So, in my mind, we both were virgins on our wedding night. I cherished that, and now my dream was shattered, my trust broken.

Jesus reminded me that He needed to be everything I wanted—my one-consuming passion. I sang through the lyrics, hopeful and soaking in the message He was giving me through this timely remembrance.

Reaching the end of the trail, I faced the second falls. They were lightly flowing, and there was easy access to hop across rocks and only get a little muddy trying to cross the water's path to climb up beside the falls. I climbed to the top of the falls and sat upon a vast flat rock overlooking them. Spreading out my journal, I settled in for writing and reflection. Inhaling the earthy tang and lush greenery, the thick foliage grew abundantly. The sound of water trickling and cascading down was invigorating. As I leaned back on the rock, I reveled in the sunlight filtering through the trees. I'd packed sidewalk chalk in case I needed to mark the trail. With it I wrote in big letters on a rock, I am a mountain mover.

God and I spent a refreshing time fellowshipping. He was there, and I could feel it. I took out my phone and took pictures. I was trying to get a picture of my True Love Waits ring and accidentally started taking a video. Instead of turning the video off, I left it on and started praying out loud.

"God, I'm here on top of this mountain. And I want this relationship with you to be more real than

anything I've known. I love you, Jesus. And I thank you for being with me my whole life. For romancing, loving, and drawing me near to you. To where I can't ever leave you. I feel you here.

And God, if you want me to climb these mountains, I will try. But you're going to have to teach me to climb. You'll have to teach me to pulverize them cause I don't know how.

Jesus, you're the love of my life. You're my faithful love. God, I want a rich, abundant life. I'm scared to death of it. The pain. The cost of that. I know when I prayed that I would love you more, that I would love Kenny, and you would teach me agape love... To love him more than I have before..... I didn't want this. But I don't have a choice. I don't have a choice. And this is the path you have called me to walk, God. But I know you're here with me, Lord and Father, if it's going to take this pain-...if it's going to take me to the next level with you.....

God, I'm going to need you every step of the way. I'm going to be angry. I'm going to be bitter. It's going to live with me for the rest of my life. It will be a daily crying out to Jesus to love and not hate. To be kind instead of uncaring or detached. To communicate when I want to stonewall. To seek you and rely on you when I want to rely on my own strength....

Today is June 21st, and Jesus, I hope, a year from now... I hope I'm going to be in a different place. I hope that my love for you and my walk with you will just be so beautiful. And I hope that Kenny and I will start to see a new change and a new thing and have a completely different relationship. But you have to show me how that's gotta look and what you want it to be, what you want it to look like, God. I love you, Jesus. I love you."

I scheduled an appointment with a tattoo artist while in Tennessee. I wanted words of truth and encouragement graven on my body. I wanted to remember I was loved, so I got the words "loved by God" on my wrist. As I sat in the tattooist's chair, we talked.

She was sweet and told me I could play any music I wanted as she worked. I played what became my Christian survival playlist. These songs became words of truth and encouragement played repeatedly to keep me going and remind me of Who was in control.

As I sat in her chair, I looked at some of the pictures she had on the wall. The one directly facing me was an artsy painting of a mountain with Latin words circling it. There it was again, another mountain reminder. I asked her what the words meant. She said it meant conquering or climbing the mountain.

On my last day at my friend's house, I returned to the hiking spot with the waterfalls. The weather forecast predicted a drizzly day, so I made a makeshift poncho out of a trash bag to protect my clothes. It had rained the night before, and as it continued to rain lightly throughout the day, the woods looked completely different. The little creek beds along the trail, which were dry only two days ago, were now flowing with water, and the waterfalls were thundering. As I approached the second waterfall, I could no longer climb up to it because the water was rushing down the creek bed that I had easily crossed before. Angling as close to the waterfall as possible, I settled down under a nearby rock overhang.

After journaling and praying for a while, the sprinkling rain made it difficult to keep my papers dry.

The echoes of voices and crunching footsteps approached. I stayed hidden in my little cave. I peeked out to see two older teen boys climbing and exploring the area, trying to get to the waterfall. They managed to get to the top of the falls, and then, after a while, they wandered off, never knowing I was there.

I gathered my things to return to the backpack and wandered off on a trail hike. Following the ascending trail, water rushed down the pathway, soaking my shoes. Undeterred, I stopped to take pictures and enjoy the little treasures I found.

Bright orange caught my eye. A fluorescent, orange-colored newt stood on his little mound of moss.

Click. He was beautiful and stood out in stark contrast to the green and brown around him.

The water flowing down the path washed a large crawdad past me. I caught him in a cup I had stuck in my pack. He looked like a miniature red lobster.

Click. I let him go and continued.

Coming to the first trail marker, I read the sign and made note of which path I planned to take. It was supposed to make a large loop and bring me out near the park office and parking lot. It looked straightforward on the map—no turns, just follow the loop. I felt confident there was no way to get lost.

Fallen trees lay over the trail at different points. Coming up on a mass of branches and trunks, I couldn't see the path beyond it. This timber completely barred my way. The terrain beside the path was steep. Crouching close to the earth, I grabbed growth growing up the hill. Hand over hand, grabbing branches, sticks, ferns, and rocks, I inched upwards.

My sneakers started to slip, and down I went, erasing my progress. I tried again, pulling hard on branches and clawing until I could gain ground.

Finally, I got around the tree and connected with the trail again. I fell multiple times. The rocks were slippery, and my legs were weary from walking. Several hours passed, and the trail continued onward.

Worry started to gnaw at me. It was getting late, and I saw no end in sight. My cell wasn't getting reception on the mountain. I had given my best friend a time frame so she could contact the park ranger if she didn't hear from me around 5 pm. After committing to hours of walking, I started thinking about bears, too. What if I met one? I'd spent so much time already. What if I had to turn around and return the way I'd come? It would be too much time to backtrack. The thoughts circled, besides the fear of falling and injury. Thankfully, I picked myself up each time and didn't seem to twist an ankle.

As I walked, I prayed or sang songs off and on. This was a powerful thing! The journey would be easier if I kept singing and worshipping. When I was silent and started to worry, the journey was difficult. As long as I kept singing, I felt God's presence and was at peace.

This was God's training ground. Through this practical life experience, God taught me a spiritual lesson that praising and trusting in Him during this journey would make it bearable. I had to fix my eyes on Him, and He would lead me through this.

Reaching a peak with an overlook, I managed to get some reception. I texted Melissa and told her I was still on the trail and to push my time frame further back. She told me to be careful; the forecast had some tornado warnings.

After walking for three hours, I still hadn't met other people on the trail. The loop didn't look long on paper, and I hoped to see the way out around the next bend.

Finally, I saw a young couple walking towards me with camping gear.

"Hi! Please tell me that the end of the trail is close." I pleaded.

"Yes, it's about maybe forty-five minutes," they replied.

I was greatly relieved to see people, and knowing my journey was about to end, I continued. After a while, I could see a sign ahead of me. But instead of comforting me, it brought dread!

There were two ways to choose from. Which way was to the parking area? *Left or right?* The sign didn't say and wasn't clear. Both ways were wooded with no indication of civilization.

I pulled out the map and still felt frustrated as it didn't indicate another path. I was so tired and just wanted this to end. My first instinct was to go left. That looked like the way to me, but after studying the map as closely as possible, I chose to go right. "Thank you, Jesus! Thank you!" I praised, finally seeing a clearing at the trail's end. I still had another twenty-minute walk to my car, but I was out of the woods! Back to civilization.

The next day, I started the eight-hour drive back home. My trip to Tennessee was valuable for me in my healing journey. I came back feeling more at peace. Although I had not yet decided to stay with my spouse permanently, I felt that it was where God wanted me to be at that time, and I was comforted knowing that God was with me through it. On the drive, I listened to my survival music playlist and sermons by Jimmy Evans with Marriage Today. Jimmy was so encouraging. He and his wife Karen had been on the edge of divorce, and God had completely changed their marriage. Jimmy made me want to believe that we could make it.

While I was away in Tennessee, Kenny struggled emotionally, waiting for my return. He continued to work but didn't know what to do on days off duty. There weren't many people Kenny could turn to for support.

We'd been going to Kingdom Life Church for the last six months, but previously, we had gone to Westminster Reformed Presbyterian in Suffolk, Virginia, for years. The Pastor there, Ruffin Alphin, had married us. We hadn't seen Ruffin for a long time since we'd visited other churches closer to us for several years.

While Kenny was alone and distraught, he walked into the church office. Ruffin observed him come in, took one look, and assessed he needed help. Taking Kenny back to his desk, they talked and prayed together.

We barely communicated while I was in Tennessee. He gave me the space I requested. He hadn't eaten since I left.

As I covered the last miles from Tennessee, I mentally tried to prepare myself. I was still uncomfortable facing him. What would I say? How do I address the elephant in the room? My cell chimed.

I'm making French dip subs for dinner. -Kenny

My favorite.

As I pulled into my parking spot, I noticed our next-door neighbor was having a big birthday celebration. Sparing no expense for her grandbaby, petting zoo animals wandered her backyard. Kenny and the kids mingled with the neighbors.

Stepping inside our house, savory hints of the roast beef warming on the stovetop greeted me.

I heard rushed footsteps behind, "Allie?!"

Panic-laced, "Have you seen Allie?" Kenny asked, tromping through the rooms.

"No, I just walked in the door."

"I just left her for five minutes and told the boys to watch her at the party while I came here to work on the subs. Now she's nowhere to be seen."

Running through the house, we searched for our four-year-old. Had she come home? Dashing to the neighbors, we combed the house and backyard, which was full of merrymakers.

Questioning those around, we discovered she had gone with another neighbor to get something from their house to return to the party. We received an apology. Most who observed probably thought we were overreacting, but they didn't know the intense emotional mess we had been through. Our nerves were already on edge. We left with our four-year-old in tow.

Back at the house, Kenny and I breathed a sigh of relief.

"Hi." He said.

I was thankful that the crazy circumstance broke the ice. It had given us something else to focus on in those first few moments. We settled in, and he ate for the first time since I'd left.

As we continued packing, we realized that our new rental had carpeting and our six-year-old chihuahua, who wasn't completely potty trained, wouldn't be a good fit. Fortunately, a friend of ours knew a family who was interested in adopting her, so Bella had a good home to go to. Ollie, our newest furry addition to the family, had been another source of stress. Ollie had been with us for about nine months. When Kenny wanted to adopt Ollie, I could sense he was trying to fill an emptiness.

However, this big boxer pit bull mix was full of issues. Though he loved us, he was super aggressive to visitors and highly anxious when we left the house. He tore up almost all our blinds throughout the house and even chewed our couch!

We got a kennel for him when we needed to leave the house, but nothing was going to stop this dog. He rammed and raged against the kennel until he forced his way through the metal and squeezed his way out.

We had to return him to the adoption company. We weren't able to meet his specific needs and challenges adequately.

Following the exodus of the dogs came the plague of fleas. Fleas that seemed to multiply by the hundreds! Ollie had slept in the children's room, the primary source from which they were coming.

We bombed the house twice in every room, and yet they lived. Both Kenny and I washed all the bedding over and over. We began washing it and then bagging it to pack it for the move. We had to take all our rugs outside and leave them as trash. I bleached the kid's toys and toy boxes. Even when we returned to the empty house months later, the fleas still came out of the floorboards to bite us!

Our anniversary on June twenty-eighth came around a week and a half after the confession. I didn't want to celebrate our anniversary that year. I went on the warpath, marching down the hall to our bedroom, Kenny hard on my heels.

"I'm going to destroy our wedding pictures!"

"No. April stop. No!" he pleaded.

Pulling out the album, I started flipping the pages. He sat on the corner of the bed, trying to talk me off the cliff.

Glancing up, I said, "I'm not going to destroy them all, but I am going to remove any pictures with her!"

Taylor attended our wedding. I removed and ripped up each picture I saw with her.

Grabbing another one, I paused. It was just her and I. Her back was to the camera, but I was facing it with my eyes closed and a smile on my face as I hugged her tightly. We were saying goodbye. It had been time to leave the wedding reception. She'd been crying as we embraced.

I chose to keep the picture, I removed it from the album, tucking it away in other memorabilia. The picture influenced a letter I would soon write to her.

The next day my sister-in-law Charlee and I sat in the car recouping from my Group Fight demonstration.

Summer heat gained in the sun's upward climb. Engine idling, I braced myself to call Taylor. Charlee was moral support. Inhale. Press call. Deep breath, ringing. Her perky voice answered, tickling my ear pressed to the receiver. Relief. Just voicemail.

"Taylor, it's April. I know. And I want you to tell your husband. It will only be a matter of time before the news comes through the grapevine. You will be receiving a letter from me stating my wishes. I love you. Bye."

I did love her, but I also wanted to hold her accountable to tell her husband the truth. I didn't want the lie to go on, but I wanted her to be the one to tell him. Ding. She texted a brief apology and said she would wait for my letter. She also asked for some time as she didn't want to tell her husband, with Father's Day being the following weekend, hoping I'd understand. She asked a few other questions. I didn't respond and blocked her number.

That evening, I wrote her a letter.

I couldn't process many feelings entirely when I wrote the letter. Had I written it later, I might have been far angrier or accusing, but I believe it was for the best that I wrote it when I did.

I told Taylor I would forgive her and that one day we would embrace as changed women in heaven, but that while we were here on this earth, she was not safe for me or my family.

I still believe in the future of peace and fellowship with her in our heavenly home. Forgiveness didn't mean I had to be in regular fellowship or best friends with her. Some people are not healthy to be with. Forgiveness frees me from the weight of anger and bitterness. However, for my marriage's health and healing, Taylor could no longer be in my circles or welcome into my fellowship.

After Father's Day, I got a text from Taylor's husband, Jimmy. Since our families had been close, Jimmy was also close to us. Jimmy's response amazed me. He apologized for her behavior, his responsibility, and his failure as her spiritual leader in controlling his household.

We commiserated with each other over the dagger of betrayal plunged into our chests. We talked about forgiveness. He must have struggled with anger towards Kenny, yet in one text, he stated he missed Ken and wished he could hug him. His grace-filled response was remarkable.

Jimmy reached out every few days. We identified with the same pain and looked for support.

I was in a very vulnerable place. Unhappy in my marriage, with a decision to make. Thoughts of "freedom" popped up.

Would I be happier with another man? Now was the time to get out. I could start over. Thoughts swirling around my mind, the temptation to reach out to other men appealing.

I'd been jealous of Taylor's beauty, sensual magnetism, and confidence; Kenny had been jealous of my admiration for Taylor's husband and his strong spiritual leadership and fun personality. Now, Kenny not only feared me leaving him for what he'd done but also that I desired other men.

I had a counseling session with Jessica by myself and shared with her these thoughts and temptations. She told me I couldn't fix or restore our marriage if I had other men on my mind, and I couldn't focus or do the work that needed to be done in our marriage.

I blocked Jimmy's number from my phone, considering how vulnerable I was and the level of emotional intimacy we were sharing through our pain.

Years prior, a similar situation arose in our marriage, I had become close to one of the pastors of a church we were attending. I had no romantic feelings for this man, but I stepped over appropriate boundaries by sharing the emotional struggles I was having. Pastoral counseling is normal, but this was based more on friendship rather than in a professional manner. I was sharing things I didn't feel I could share with my husband.

At that point in our marriage, I felt disconnected from Kenny, both spiritually and emotionally, so I confided in this pastor. Kenny was uncomfortable with this, so I would hide or delete texts between the pastor and me.

Kenny wanted us out of that church. He tried to talk to the pastor about the situation and lay out his rules and boundaries, but I was embarrassed and begged him not to. Many people, including the pastor, didn't understand why we left. But I had learned my lesson about getting too emotionally intimate with other men.

I also went through and unfriended men on Facebook. Kenny and I agreed not to befriend people of the opposite sex on Facebook going forward.

This was difficult for neighbors and church people we met, as most people don't use Facebook that way, but we tried to be consistent with this rule as much as possible.

I also had a list of rules for Kenny, as he destroyed many boundaries. He changed his email and phone number and deleted apps that Taylor and he used. He gave me access to all his accounts and blocked her from all his social media sites.

He included tracking on our cell phones so I could see his location anytime. Our phones were open if we wanted to look.

Your Journey, Your Story

Your life has just turned upside down, so you may not feel like singing songs or praising God. But did you know there is power in worship for healing? Worship takes our focus off our circumstances and directs our focus to the One who is our Hope.

Why is worship important? It can lift our spirits during our deepest, darkest moments. In some of the Bible's most amazing stories of deliverance, God stepped in where worship came first.

Even if your spirit is too overwhelmed to sing, listen. Song lyrics can speak truth, hope, comfort, and peace to troubled souls. Make a survival playlist of songs that encourage your soul and keep you going.

When we are in that pit and don't see a way out, worship invites the presence of God. It invites the Holy Spirit to do what we can't do in our own power.

Some of the Psalms, are David's songs. He wrote them in the thick of difficult situations. He cried out to God, sharing his feelings and frustrations, but he ended the song with faith in God and remembering how God had provided before.

We may not feel like praising or thanking God, but can we stop and see the blessings in these moments? Can we find something to be thankful for each day?

Gratitude is a posture God can work mightily with. In those early days of recovery, I thanked God for the moment-by-moment that he sustained me. I thanked Him for His presence, for friends and support. I thanked Him for being my confidant and, most importantly, faithful. My spouse wasn't faithful, but God was.

Questions to Consider

What songs and scriptures lift you during this time? What can you thank God for in this moment?

Frozen Head State Park

A Wife's Recovery from an Affair-69

A Wife's Recovery from an Affair-70

I AM a
MOUNTAIN
MOVER

April & Taylor on April's wedding day

4

First Step to Forgiveness

Dusk fell as we finished packing our garage during our final week in Franklin. Emotion still heavily weighed on me. I went to the swing set in the backyard, I glided back and forth under the starry sky.

Growing up, one of my comforts and joys was swinging and singing at the top of my lungs. The stars always beckoned me, and I loved the feeling of a warm summer night.

One of the survival songs I'd clung to was "Spirit of the Living God" by Meredith Andrews. Turning the song up on my phone, I sang along.

I could feel the Holy Spirit's presence, begging Him to come and make a change in my heart that only He could do. I couldn't change my marriage alone, and I couldn't forgive, but He could. My heart was prideful, angry, and hurt, but I wanted to see what God saw.

Moving to the swing beside me, Kenny sat silently, listening to the song and being present. He asked if he could play a song that greatly affected him.

I listened as Matthew West's "Mended" played into the night.

The song Mended was healing for Kenny. Feeling broken and used after experiencing sexual abuse as a child, he carried the shame and weight of it throughout his life. He felt like damaged goods.

Now, he also had the weight of the affair. But as he sought after God, the Holy Spirit spoke the words of life he needed to hear. He was a precious child of God, loved, mended, redeemed, and headed toward hope. He'd been a prisoner of his past and the lies he believed. But the Holy Spirit brought a man in deep darkness and sin into great hope and healing.

I witnessed the changes God had made in Kenny's heart and life throughout those last months, but the acknowledgment of the affair shattered my certainty in his genuineness and fear of his future commitment to Jesus. However, when he shared this song, it helped me to see where he was coming from and what the words meant to him.

Moving day arrived. A few family members and a couple from church helped load the van. Eager to get on the road, I went ahead in my car to meet them at our new house. Kenny drove the van, while our friends from church followed behind in their vehicle.

I received a call. Kenny was broken down. I was twenty-five minutes further down the road, I whipped the car around, angry and frustrated.

About thirty minutes into their trip, our friends noticed that the back of the moving van was weaving. Kenny pulled over to a gas station to inspect the van and assessed it was too dangerous to drive and needed to be fixed.

The rental company promised to send a repairer to check out the van. So, we sat and waited. I called two family members who were supposed to meet us at the new place to unload and told them we were delayed.

My nerves were on edge. Raw and tired from packing, fighting fleas, and battling the instability of emotions that gushed out after the confession, my endurance was fading.

This move seemed foreboding, and the setback made me feel even more unsure about everything. I sat in the car while Kenny and our friends debated what to do.

Tears slipped down my cheeks. My oldest son was aware that I was not ok.

"Mom, what's wrong?"

"Mama is just still hurting."

"How did Daddy break your heart? What did he say that hurt you? Did he love another woman?" He asked.

I held him in my lap. He had guessed it. I didn't want to answer his question, as the connection with our families would make it difficult and produce more questions, so I just held him close.

Time ticked by. It was getting close to dinner time, and the mechanic still hadn't shown up. We had a pizza dinner from the gas station convenience store outside on a picnic table.

Kenny sensed my glum attitude and tried to make things light and occupy the children. As the hours dragged on, I was so thankful for our friends from church who stayed with us. They offered their support and truly kept me sane. The pressing emotions would have crushed me if they hadn't been there.

We began discussing options for the night as it became clear we couldn't get to the new house and unpack that day. We couldn't go to either home because neither had furniture or beds. Our friends offered to let us come back and stay with them. A hotel was not too far away, so we decided to stay there to be closer if Kenny needed to meet with the mechanic.

Because of the delay, I was anxious and stressed about getting help unloading the moving van. Our help couldn't come the next day, so I posted on Facebook asking for prayers and requesting help.

A friend I had not seen since high school lived within an hour of our new home and offered to come. I was so thankful and relieved that God had provided.

We checked into our hotel room for the night. The room had two sections. In the living area, we set up a cot and pull-out couch for our boys and kissed them goodnight. Shutting the door to their room, we settled into ours.

I felt angry, resentful, and withdrawn. Lying beside him in bed, we talked but ended up getting into a discussion that made me bitter and accusatory. Sinking into vengeful feelings and temptations, I rolled out of bed and put on some jeans.

"What are you doing? Where are you going?" He asked, sitting up in bed.

"I don't know, maybe I'll go find a bar somewhere and flirt to see if someone will take me home," I said clenching my fists.

He stood and bared my way to the door.

"April, don't do anything stupid. Don't do that. Do you think it will make you feel better? Do you think this is a game? It isn't good. It's awful. And you'll regret it just like I did."

"Get out of my way!" I said, glaring at him, planting myself in a stiff stance. I tried at the door, but he pushed his body against it so I couldn't open it.

"Let me out! I'm going to go crazy in here! I don't want to be here another minute with you!" I spat out.

Fury rose inside me again, just like it had in the car. *Trapped again. I'm going to explode.* Like a deer in the headlights, he feared my words and erratic behavior.

I have to let go of this rage. I must get out now before I unleash on him again.

Turning away from the door, I balled up my fists, screaming and slamming my fists violently on the hotel mattress. Mercilessly, I slammed my upper body and fists against the mattress over and over.

Weight forced me down. Warm mass pressing against me. Kenny's body weight kept me from being able to move. Crying and praying, he pleaded again,

"Baby, please stop."

He wouldn't release me until I promised to stop fighting. Slowly, the heaviness lifted, "April, please promise me you won't do anything stupid."

"I don't know, I just need to get out of here." I walked out the door, tiptoeing through the dark room where the boys slept, Kenny sobbed from the other side of the doorway. My heart cold, I made strides through the hallway and to the hotel parking lot.

I shook from adrenaline, like a tiger pacing its cage, a tumble of feelings. I didn't know what to do, so I just started walking in circles in the parking lot.

I needed to pray, but I was so upset that I didn't have the mind or strength to pray. I shakily dialed Melissa's number. I told her what had happened and that I needed her to pray. As she began, I continued walking and just listened. She said everything I could not—asking for love and forgiveness, my husband, strength, and grace in the move. She continued for about thirty minutes. It was helping.

Slowly, the intensity of my anger and feelings calmed. I felt God there. He was there even in my lack of godliness and my sinful failure. He was helping me. Hanging up with her, I continued to pray and walk.

After spending another hour outside, feeling exhausted, I returned to the hotel room. Kenny was sitting on the bed, praying and reading his Bible. I ignored him, turned off the light, and crawled into the other double bed, turning my back to him. I could hear him crying. Coldly, I told him to be quiet and go to sleep. I was being unnecessarily mean, and I knew it.

After tossing and turning, unable to relax because I could sense his emotion and unrest, I told him to crawl in bed beside me.

The following day, we arrived at the house. We were told the U-Haul had been towed to our new place during the night. However, it wasn't there. After calling around, Kenny found out that it was on the way. Thankfully, it came in time with the extra help God provided.

My high school friend even brought everyone pizzas, drinks, and cookies! They were such a blessing to us. The couple from church who had been our moral support the day before came out to help. Several of Kenny's new co-workers came too.

We spent the night in our new house, but I returned to our old church the following Sunday, staying with my parents and sister-in-law Charlee for several days. Still hurting and indecisive, I wanted to be near family for support. Charlee and I walked along a country road one evening in the fading sun.

"April, do you feel that God brought Kenny into your life to grow, walk with, and help you become more like Christ?" she asked.

I pondered this. Yes, I'd considered this a training ground for growing more like Jesus, but I kept coming back to my selfish and sinful desires.

Did I want to change? The truth was that though Kenny was responsible for his actions, I hadn't created a healthy marriage environment either. Many of my sinful habits of selfishness, stonewalling, pride, unforgiveness, and detachedness in marriage had not helped my spouse feel loved.

Through the years, I had pushed him away in many ways. The thought bothered me: If I haven't changed in fourteen years of marriage, how am I supposed to now?

A part of me wanted to believe it would be different with someone else, that someone else could make me happier, and that these sin issues of mine would go away if I really loved the other person. Maybe Kenny and I weren't meant for each other.

It was the last week before summer school began for our kids in our new town. Once summer school started, I would be stuck in Fredericksburg until they finished those two school weeks. I stayed with my mom again to have space to think and pray. I wanted to have some of these questions answered. I tried to decide whether I was leaving or staying. My Aunt

Janet and Uncle Brad from Connecticut had come to Virginia to visit the extended family, and I talked and prayed with them. My aunt was one of the godliest women I knew, and I greatly respected her advice as a pastor's wife. She recommended the book, "What Did You Expect?" by Paul David Tripp.

I dove into this book the last week I had at my mom's house. It convicted me and the way I viewed my spouse and my marriage.

Sitting upon the porch swing overlooking the plowed field in front of my mother's house, I dialed my aunt.

"Janet, I read the book but have some more questions. Do you think God meant for Kenny and me to be together?"

She was never one to answer hastily, her response weighing the words with solemn regard.

"I believe God had a plan and purpose when He brought you two together."

"With all the trouble and unhappiness we've had in our marriage, do you think I could have a better marriage with someone else? Would it be easier that way rather than trying to stay?"

Her soft reply was, "You might choose to be with someone who doesn't have the same flaws Kenny has, but there would still be things about this new person you wouldn't like and would have to choose to live with.

April, we all bring baggage into the marriage. Though I chose to marry your uncle, and there were things I liked about him, later, some of those things became differences that were frustrations. If you marry someone else, you may get rid of some baggage Kenny had, but that new person would have a different set of baggage and differences to work through.

No matter who you marry, you will still carry your shortcomings and failures into a new relationship. You will both disappoint each other and fail, but that is why you have to cling to Jesus. April, we serve Christ by serving each other, dying to our kingdoms and plans, and submitting to each other and God's Kingdom purposes."

After hanging up, I stood in the grassy yard, feeling at peace. I received assurance and a godly perspective.

After putting the kids to bed in my mother's guest rooms, I walked into the night for an evening prayer walk. My guides were no streetlights with country living, The Milky Way, and a sliver of the moon.

My footsteps crunched on the gravel driveway, and a symphony of crickets could be heard from the shadows of the trees.

My purpose? Start forgiving.

"I forgive Kenny for cheating on me. I forgive him for having sex with her. I forgive him for spending money on her. I forgive him for lying to me. I forgive him for loving her." I continued, naming everything Kenny did that hurt me.

I prayed for Taylor. I forgave her for betraying me, for lying to me, for taking from me what was mine. I prayed for her spiritual restoration, her walk with God, and her marriage.

The truth is that forgiveness is a process. But it had to start somewhere. That was naming every offense and verbally declaring that I chose to forgive them. It was a freeing feeling.

But I also knew I couldn't leave Kenny in the dark about my decision. Slipping into my guest room, I called him.

"Hello?"

I quietly said, "I forgive you."

"Thank you, Baby," he choked out. I could hear him crying on the other side of the line.

"This is going to take a process, Kenny. I will probably have moments I get angry and still hurt, but I will continually try to forgive you as things come up."

The first day of summer school arrived. We took the boys to the bus stop. I was feeling nervous. We had many concerns with the boys as they had both been homeschooled.

I had taken them as far as I could in my teaching ability. We had hit learning barriers, and I hoped they would get the help they needed from the teachers in Stafford.

Their concerns weren't as noticeable. They were smiling and excited to ride a bus. We went to the school around noon to have lunch and check out library books with them. The principal knew each child's name. It was incredible how he could remember so many names and faces personally reaching out to the kids and their families.

The children's teachers dove right into getting the extra tutoring and help the kids needed to succeed. This was a huge answer to prayer for me as it was another thing weighing on my mind with all that was going on.

Finishing lunch at the school, we got our beach stuff and headed to a little sandy spot by the river, only about five minutes from the house. We were thrilled by this free "beach" and enjoyed swimming and playing in the sand by the riverside.

I was seeing God's provision in many ways. In our townhouse neighborhood, a trail led off into the woods. Wild roses and wildflowers grew along the trail. Having a nature trail near where I could walk and pray was a blessing.

Prayer walking has been a part of my life since my teenage years. I have always sought out natural places to enjoy this activity, and I have found that God has always provided such places for me, no matter where we have moved. Finding a good church was also vital to us. Without family close by, we needed a strong support group. Our church needed to be our family. Through a mutual friend who had a connection with someone in our area, she suggested trying Crossroads Church. We were invited to attend their worship night, we eagerly jumped on the front row. After the service, a woman my age named Priscylla came up to welcome me and ask how long I'd been coming to Crossroads. We both had recently moved to the Fredericksburg area and were moms trying to connect with people there.

She was so sweet and gave me her phone number. She told me about summer pop-ups, a way the church did fellowship that summer. Anyone could post a cookout, park playdate, or event as an open invitation for people in the church to join. I dove right in and started marking my calendar with numerous parties and activities that were offered.

My first trip was to a fire station with other moms from church. We took our kids, and they saw the fire trucks and held the water hose while it was pumping. I'd hoped Priscylla would be there that day, but she wasn't. I socialized with as many moms as I could.

I felt lonely those first few weeks trying to get plugged in, especially when Kenny was at work. Some days, weighed with depression, I didn't want to get out of bed. I would pray and rise, trying to busy myself with tasks. Appreciating the closeness of the townhouses, I'd chat with neighbors, wanting to be around people.

I posted an invite to our house for a women's painting night on the neighborhood Facebook page. I had the supplies and could give an introductory painting lesson. A few people were interested in coming, but the night I had it, no one came.

I baked homemade goods and took them door to door to meet the neighbors. We also invited seven neighbors to dinner. All of them came.

The prior renter had caused a lot of drama and had some illegal drug dealings, so they were relieved that we seemed like an average family. One of our female neighbors asked how Kenny and I met.

It's strange how we have coping mechanisms and ways of detaching. I talked about us in a rosy way, truly remembering the magic of how we met.

I met Kenny at a church picnic. I thought I had scoped all the guys out at church and decided no one was there for me.

I didn't have a great sense of style at that point in my life, but even I knew that my flowered overalls, which came up mid-calf because they were too short, with white socks and tennis shoes, were a fashion nightmare.

While playing volleyball with some younger kids, this hunk introduced himself to me. The first things I noticed were his blue eyes and manly hands.

This was no boy; this was a man. Aware of my poor style choice, I had no idea why this handsome dude was even talking to me. In the time it took to shake his hand in greeting, I had already taken him down the wedding aisle in my mind.

At this point in my story, my neighbor exclaimed, "Aw, you found the perfect guy. And you lived happily ever after!" I smiled and laughed it off.

We had a good night getting to know our neighbors. One commented how sweet it was that I had brought baked goods to everyone and invited them over. "That's what we should have done to welcome you to the neighborhood." She said.

I knew what I was doing was backward, but my neighbors didn't know how desperate I was to make friends. I wasn't waiting for a handout or offer of friendship from others. I was going to charge in and make it happen on my own. I didn't have time to sit and wait for people to initiate courtesy and relationships; I was bleeding out.

The next church event I attended was a cultural night. The host, Myrna, came from a Latino culture. Friendly, with rich curly locks and amazing cooking skills, she made everyone feel at home.

Guests brought food to share. Many of the courses were traditional dishes from other countries. My plate was piled with unique cuisine; I settled at a table on their screened-in porch.

Knowing hardly anyone, I contentedly observed, listening to the conversations around me. My attention kept coming back to one person.

Her name was Diana. She was a native of Mexico who had recently moved to the States. She appeared younger than me and had been newly married for only about a month.

My heart went out to her, knowing that she was miles and miles from family and unable to drive at the time because of paperwork issues.

While her husband worked, she was alone at home in a strange city. She barely spoke English.

Our eyes kept meeting, and I smiled warmly at her. I decided I wanted to get to know her. I felt a kindred spirit. I reasoned that if she were new here too, like Priscylla, I would have a better chance of becoming friends with someone who needed a friend rather than someone already rooted in relationships.

The following week, I invited Myrna and Diana to visit. I was a little worried that I would feel left out as both spoke Spanish, but Myrna was an excellent translator, and they included me in conversations. Their sweet fellowship and kindness made my heart whole.

While trying to pour myself into connecting with others, I struggled to connect fully with Kenny. He continued to pursue me and try to get close to me, and it was just hard to open myself up to him.

We continued to work on the "Torn Asunder" workbook. Some of the exercises involved learning things about each other that you didn't know about your spouse growing up. We were also supposed to share monologues about specific time frames from our lives.

We had our first official date a month after the confession and did one of the monologues between dinner and dessert. We set up a canopy over our back porch and had a nice dinner.

We worked on a different chapter in the workbook every two weeks and had a session with Jessica to discuss our progress. In these lessons, I learned that many of the contributing factors and negative vibes in the marriage were my fault.

One of the big projects we worked on was writing forgiveness letters. I was to write one about the hurt I had caused in the marriage.

I read my letter to Kenny and saw the pain on his face as I confessed specific things that had deeply hurt him, like an arrow piercing his heart. It was sobering and eye-opening to realize how broken we had been and the unhealthy things I had contributed.

He read his letter to me, which was equally emotional. We both cried as we read to each other and asked for forgiveness.

Kenny showed emotion frequently remembering the hurt he had caused me. Strangely I couldn't cry very much. I wanted to cry. To release the chaotic thoughts and feelings inside, but it took a while before I could regularly cry and grieve.

After about a month of living in the Stafford area, we decided to call Crossroads our church home. Even though Kenny had fallen into sin with the affair, he was fully repentant and was striving hard after God at the time. He had the heart to lead a small group of men at our church. However, we didn't know what our pastors would think about that.

We made an appointment to come to the church office and tell them our story. Upfront and honest we asked how they would feel if Kenny led a group, especially where we were in our healing. Pastor Joel only had one concern.

"How strong do you feel your marriage is right now?"

He wanted to know that we would not sacrifice our healing or work that needed to happen between us.

Kenny answered affirmingly. I still had some unsteady feelings, but I wanted to support him in this. I could see his gifts as a teacher and wanted him involved in something spiritually eternal and valuable. The pastors gave us their blessing.

The church had another worship night a few weeks later. We stood worshiping on the front row, a woman we didn't know by name and who didn't know our story tapped Kenny on the back.

"Excuse me, while you both were worshipping, I felt like God wanted me to tell you that He is making all things new," the stranger said. We both exchanged glances and started to get teary-eyed. She continued to speak more directly to Kenny.

"You feel like you aren't good. The man you are now is not the man you were. People will look at you and say, Is that the same person?" These words were healing to Kenny. All the grief and shame he felt over the affair tore at him.

She shared how she'd been a sinful, terrible person, and then God completely changed her. This was one of those moments when we could clearly hear God speak through others, affirming that He was working, He was healing, He was restoring.

Your Journey, Your Story

Forgiveness is a big piece of healing. Right now, it may seem absolutely impossible, but it is necessary. Forgiving someone doesn't mean that what they did was okay. Forgiveness is letting go of having to be their judge. Unforgiveness is a burden that will continue to snowball and make you bitter and angry, making it impossible to heal fully. Forgiveness truly frees you from clenching onto this burden.

If you have decided you are willing to try, that's the first step. The next step is to speak forgiveness or write it. When I prayed to forgive my spouse, did I truly feel forgiving? Did I feel ready to hold him in my arms and say, "Okay, I'm good. We're fine. Let's move on?" No, but it was the first step to verbalizing and choosing forgiveness.

Forgiveness is a choice, not a feeling. I chose to forgive, and I chose to do it again and again when the reminders and emotions come up. Forgiveness is a process.

What if your spouse is not repentant? Forgiveness will be even harder if there is no repentance.

Counseling is advised, especially if the spouse is unwilling to apologize or repent.

Forgiveness also doesn't mean restoration has to occur. We can forgive someone, but we do not have to allow them to have the same role in our lives as they had before.

Even if you and your spouse cannot reconcile to stay married, forgiveness will free you. There is no denying that this is a difficult thing to do. Jesus Christ poured himself out for others, and his closest followers betrayed him. He was abandoned by his friends and killed on a cross by people who had praised him and then turned on him. Jesus knows what it is like to forgive in the face of deep hurt.

All of us have sinned against God. No matter how we have sinned and turned away from Him, God has forgiven us. If we want to walk with Him, we have to be able to forgive others.

This is something we can't do on our own. It requires the Holy Spirit's strength and power. If you are willing, that is when the Holy Spirit can work. He can use our weaknesses and give us the power to do the impossible.

Gas station pizza dinner after moving van broke down.

5

Intimacy & Rebuilding

Summer school ended for the boys, and we tried to make the most of our quickly ending summer by taking a camping trip to Pennsylvania. I worried about the close quarters and our being together in the same tent, but since so much had already happened that summer, camping was one of the only options for last-minute vacation planning.

The weather was great, and we settled into our wooded spot. We visited the Hershey factory, went hiking, and swam in the campground's pool with a waterslide. Our boys made us laugh because they went down the waterslide for two hours.

One night, after we all went to bed, I was emotional, and I remember Kenny holding me as I quietly cried. We were trying to live normally and reconnect, but the pain was still there. It ended up being a great trip and a helpful distraction from reality.

Getaways always meant fun sexual intimacy. The first time we sexually reconnected, we were hurting and starved for that connection. I could feel a difference. There had been a wall between us before I knew about the affair. But now, the wall was down, and I could feel our bond again.

I knew that oral sex had been a part of their sexual involvement. That hurt me the most because that had always been a special part of our union. Though we renewed our sexual intimacy after the confession, it was a while before I allowed oral sex to play a role. It was too vulnerable, and I emotionally couldn't handle it.

I had heavily prized sex and the exclusiveness of it. It was sacred to me and a relief to know that the most intimate parts of ourselves and our sexuality were not shared. I had never had any other sexual partners, and because I chose to abstain from pornography as well, I had no image to pull up or distract from our union. Now, I had pictures of them in my mind.

During our union, she was there. Thoughts of them together would pop up, which was challenging to deal with. I tried to push the thoughts away. Our counselor helped us by telling us to focus on each other in the here and now and in the moments of intimacy. Still, for several months, that was a regular battle.

I still struggled with insecurity. Was she better than me? Did he like her sex more? I did not want to verbalize or ask these questions because I dreaded the answer.

One of the ways she tried to lure and entice him was to say, "Let's see who the better kisser is, her or me?" Kenny spoke confirmation to me that he loved my mouth and my kisses. That ended up being very healing for me.

However, sex had always been an idol for me. It was good that I wanted sex within the bounds of God's design, but I would control and manipulate to get it. I wanted it on my terms and in my timing. We were also trying to pray and work through this with my healing.

During the last summer weeks, our family enjoyed day trips to various parks and nearby tourist sites, exploring our new area.

It was refreshing that no one besides our pastors knew our story. In one way, it was easier being in our new place. It brought a sense of normalcy.

However, I did feel the need to share what I was going through. To do that, I needed to establish a relationship base before sharing something so personal.

In early September 2017, I attended a Propel Women's conference with Diana and friends from church, still hiding this burden inside. We eagerly stood on the sidewalk in the long line, chattering women shuffling through the doors of the church, posing for pictures by the backdrop, and going into the auditorium to find a seat.

The worship was incredible; I was so open to wholly wanting to enter God's presence during opportunities like this that I would do whatever it took to be undistracted. Standing at my seat, I felt restricted. I wanted to be close to the altar to bow and pray. Walking up the aisle to the front row, I knelt near empty seats. Nothing blocked my view of the stage, but my face was buried in prayer and expectancy on the floor.

When the music ended and everyone was preparing to sit, I stood, and a woman smiled warmly at me and gave me a bear hug. I returned the hug and then went back to my seat. About a half hour later, this woman who had hugged me walked out on stage.

I'd been embraced by Lisa Harper, one of the speakers for the event!

I thought that was pretty cool. It was again another small blessing God was sending my way, and quite literally, it was a hug from heaven.

Diana and I continued to bond. She invited our family to a lake with other friends from her husband's work. Although they all had roots in different countries, they warmly invited us into their circle.

We loved the Latino flare of their beach celebration. They brought their grill and cooked amazing food, hung hammocks, and took turns going out on the lake with a canoe that Eddie, Diana's husband, had brought for everyone to enjoy.

Diana and I continued to try our best to improve our communication. Despite my lack of Spanish and her broken English, I could feel her heart. That was all that mattered to me. They made us feel like family, which was healing for me.

Several weekends later, the kids and I went on another adventure to a pumpkin farm with this group. Kenny was at work.

Sitting on the hayride and running through the fields looking for the perfect pumpkin, the thought again struck me. I felt at home. God was putting people in my life to lift the loneliness and was making this new place feel homier.

I was still pursuing Priscylla but had been unsuccessful at getting her alone. I finally tried to be direct and asked if we could hang out at her house. I wanted to get her alone so I could talk, ready to share my burden.

She was warm and welcoming. Our younger ones played on the floor together. We sat on her couch as I told her our story. She listened, asked questions, and prayed over me.

She shared a devotional she read that morning.

"You are like a vase, April, and it may be broken, but God is putting you back together. God can use you. The scars you have now can help someone else. You will be put together in a beautiful masterpiece for God's glory."

"As I try to make sense of this, I hope that God will use this for good, to help someone else." I said.

Kay, one of our church friends, also came over to Priscylla's later that day. I told her my story, and she shared her own. I began to see that by opening up to women, almost everyone I was vulnerable with had their own story of pain or difficulty.

Behind all the beautifully curated posts on Facebook depicting seemingly perfect and happy lives, there was a depth to every woman that I couldn't see. There was something real, raw, and beyond the surface that was buried underneath. I yearned to connect with others in that authentic way. I wanted to start blogging about my affair recovery. I had never been a writer or had any experience with technical things like a blog site, but I wanted to write and make it accessible to women going through the same thing I was. I picked an alias name and started a free blog on WordPress.

I had already processed a few things after the affair, so I wrote on different topics about affair recovery from my own experience. Not wanting to post my blog on my Facebook page, I made pins on Pinterest, which was how I started getting some readers.

When I got notifications that people had pinned my blog, I would try to message the women through Pinterest. I wanted to let them know that I was praying for them even if I didn't know where they were in their healing. Through this, I connected with two women who were in far worse situations than me.

One woman held out for her spouse while he was still with the other woman. She firmly believed God wanted them to be together. It was tough for her to be on her own, but she faithfully prayed for her husband to see the light and come back to her.

She was alone in this struggle, as most people felt she should forget him and move on. It was hard to comprehend, but I knew I couldn't argue with what God was impressing upon her heart, so I joined her in praying for the restoration of her marriage. I made sure to check in with her from time to time to see how she was doing. Another woman divorced her husband after he left her for the other woman. A year after the divorce, he pursued her again and pleaded with her to forgive him and take him back. This woman still loved her husband very much, but she also was in so much pain from all that he had done during the affair. We had multiple email conversations about her feelings and struggles. I tried to answer her questions and share my experience, but it gave me a sobering perspective.

The experience of each affair story is unique, involving different types of affairs, levels of emotional involvement, and varying degrees of pain. The healing process varies for everyone, and some individuals may find it difficult to cope with the emotional pain. Our stories were vastly different, but it was comforting to share with people who understood—people who had been through it.

As I wrote, I found healing mainly because I could see God's hand in each situation, recognizing where I had been and what he had brought me through. Sharing my experiences brought meaning and purpose to my pain, even though the traffic on my site was just numbers and not actual people with whom I got to interact. I simply hoped that maybe it was helping someone. We were all doing well. The kids were excelling in school with the help of extra tutoring to improve their grades. I was teaching kickboxing and Zumba at a gym, and Kenny was settling into his job at the fire department. He and I continued to date each other.

On one date, we walked downtown Fredericksburg and had a Facebook contest to see who could get the most likes for the best pictures. We took pictures of buildings, graffiti, sunsets, and landscapes and collaged our top four pictures. We posted the photos without telling who took which set and let the voting begin. Kenny's were more artistic in the capturing process, and mine were more colorful. My pictures got the most votes. It was silly but a fun, lighthearted activity for a date.

On another date, I got adventurous, and we tried an escape room. We were terrible at it, but it was still fun trying to work together and break through several boxes and rooms to solve the clues. On another adventure, we walked through a Garden of Lights for the holidays.

That Thanksgiving, Kenny was on duty. Our families back home were missing the grandkids and asked to have them on their fall break. We obliged. Kenny was sad to be away from family, so I chose to stay in Fredericksburg to see him at the station that day.

The station's Thanksgiving dinner wasn't until later that evening, so I went to see Kay, a friend from church and spent the morning and early afternoon with her and her family, who were in for the holiday.

We made crafts at her table and visited. God was comforting me and providing a family for me right where I was. I left before their mealtime and had dinner with Kenny at his station.

We walked and talked about all we were thankful for that year and the work we could see God doing in our marriage.

God has done a lot in our lives since the confession.

In the early days, I had painful thoughts almost constantly. I remember feeling a sense of relief about two weeks after sharing my feelings. Going to a Zumba training session provided a blessed break for my mind. I just wanted to feel normal and secure and not constantly think about the affair. Some days, I might get by with nothing more than a fleeting thought, but reminders still came up.

Simple things like knowing someone with the same name as Taylor were triggers. We did know someone here by that name, and for a while, it seemed necessary to clarify by using both the first and last names of that person, so we didn't confuse them.

Sometimes, insecurities and thoughts of comparison came up for me. I'm not sure how some women deal with this if they don't know what the other woman looks like. It was hard for me because I knew Taylor and had always felt inadequate in a physical sense to her.

Whether you see the affair partner or not, it is tempting to feel insufficient or defeated. I tried to take comfort in the fact that Kenny still chose me. That he realized what he was throwing away in our relationship.

One morning, I woke from a dream about him having another affair. Most of my dreams were wacky and crazy, but this one felt so real. I remembered thinking my dad was right, that I shouldn't trust him again, and now what would I do? I was trying to figure out where I would live and how to start over. The anger and the pain I felt in the dream was so intense. Upon waking, I was glad it was not my reality, but I felt the residual doubts and fears. Was I foolish to trust him again?

I did my devotions that morning and bowed in prayer over the bed. My husband came in from his shift work and bent beside me. I told him about the dream, and we just held each other, cried, and prayed.

These moments could feel overwhelming, but talking through them and praying together was healing. It helped us with bonding and enabled him to see the pain he had caused me.

Later that day, I still had lingering thoughts over the dream and whether I was foolish to trust him.

I pondered that question. There were no guarantees that it wouldn't ever happen again. Kenny's character had significantly changed, and a deep relationship with Jesus was a significant factor in his living with integrity. Was this still a bad decision? I believed this was the path God wanted me to walk, so I put my trust in God.

What if Kenny had another affair? Would I choose to live my life expecting the worst and not trust God with the outcome? It would be hard if it happened, but God would never forsake me. I am never alone.

So, as I drove home from work with the remnants of the dream bugging me, I returned to my survival playlist. The song I needed to hear was "Do It Again."

I believed He would make a way. When I was afraid to move forward, He made a way for us and moved this mountain.

Your Journey, Your Story

Should I stay or leave? This is one of the most sought-after answers after an affair. We want to know if we should stay in this marriage. Can we make this work, or do we need to walk away?

The emotions are so strong in the early stages of affair recovery. It can seem impossible to work through this or to conceive it working. But your attitude and your spouses will impact the fruitfulness of trying to rebuild.

Does your spouse show repentance? Is your spouse willing to go to counseling? Is your spouse willing to end the affair relationship if they are still involved? Is your spouse willing to get accountability? Do they want to work on restoring the marriage?

If so, he needs to be willing to set boundaries. Is he willing to block her number or change his? Change emails, get an accountability partner? Is he willing to have a joint Facebook account?

Pray and seek godly counsel. This is a big decision. However, you do *not* need to decide today.

Give yourself grace and time to consider and allow God to work.

Propel women's conference. April, Priscylla, Diana

One of our dates during the healing process.

6

Will the Tears Stop

The week of Christmas I was haunted by memories. The holiday season reminded me that he had been with her the year before.

This year, 2017, Kenny's duty schedule fell on Christmas Eve and Christmas Day. We opened presents with the kids the day before Christmas Eve.

On Christmas Eve, Kay hosted several families from church to come for lunch. I took the kids, and we visited, played games, and sang carols.

I went to Diana's for Christmas Eve dinner. Her in-laws from Puerto Rico were also there. Though her mother-in-law couldn't speak English with my daughter, they still sat and played together, smiling and laughing. Diana and Eddie had a gift for each of the children, and my heart warmed with their friendship and hospitality.

Christmas morning, I drove the kids to see my family. Family members slowly arrived, so I bundled up to walk into the woods.

The swampy terrain had numerous dead trees barely standing. As a teen, I enjoyed exploring the woods and occasionally kicking down rotting trunks. Feeling playful, the game was to see how many trees I could fall with one karate kick. Several sprung back, knocking me off my feet. They had stronger roots than they appeared. But a few went down with a satisfying crack and a crash.

That day, memories came back of two Christmases earlier and an early morning phone call to Taylor. She seemed to be walking closely with God at the time. I had risen early and gone for a prayer walk on my parent's country property. She texted to wish me a Merry Christmas.

Realizing she was awake, which would have been around four am her time, I leaned against a fence post to call her, and suddenly, it gave way. Stunned, I was lying on the fence, which was now on the ground.

I laughed, took a picture, and sent it to her. She answered the phone, and we talked briefly and prayed together that morning. It was one of my good memories of her before everything changed.

This Christmas was somewhat awkward as all my extended family knew about the affair. It was an elephant in the room that wasn't discussed or brought up.

What bothered me the most was the brokenness between my dad and Kenny. Kenny and my mom had been able to talk and embrace during those first few weeks after the confession. But my dad had felt betrayed and had chosen to withdraw.

Now, it had been nearly six months since either one had seen each other or spoken a word. I tried to corner my dad one of the nights I was there.

"Dad, I need to ask you to do something for me."

"What?"

"You and Kenny need to talk."

"I don't need to talk to him. There's nothing to say; he broke my trust. You forgave him, so I'll be civil to him. But we don't need to talk about anything. I might get angry."

"That's ok. Tell him how you feel. But yes, you do need to talk to each other. The ice needs to be broken; I don't want more months to go by without you saying anything to each other."

Dad half grunted an ok.

I left the kids with Mom and Dad for a few days and returned home to spend time with Kenny. He had a few days off, so we went hiking in the Shenandoah Mountains.

There were frigid temps, snow falling, and wind that cut right through you. Stuffed in double-layer clothing and wrapped with scarves around our mouths and noses, we searched for a waterfall.

Finding one, we went off trail to come alongside it to get pictures at different angles and heights. Icicles hung from rocky outcroppings. Taking photos of the waterfall inspired one of my blog posts, "Breaking the Ice After the Confession."

We returned to pick up the kids from my parents.

Dad made small talk and acted like nothing happened. It was difficult as the kids were playing, and not much could be said as they still did not know about the affair.

Kenny said, "You and I need to discuss something."

"No, we don't."

"Yes, we do." Kenny insisted and proceeded to apologize.

Dad said that he forgave him because I had, but that trust had been broken, and he wouldn't easily give him trust again.

The short interaction was a start.

We learned that sometimes those closest to us cannot handle news of an affair. For our parents, it was difficult to bear this and to respond. It was healthy for us to establish space in our healing.

I do believe that our move was the best decision for us. In many ways, it was a fresh start. As the pain of the affair also affected our families, it was healing to be around others who were further removed from that effect and thus were able to be the support we needed.

My only regret was wanting our families to see the change I saw in Kenny and our marriage. God was doing amazing things, and we grew and changed so much.

We rang in the 2018 New Year at Myrna's with friends from church. All our families and little ones were together, playing games and hanging out.

The Sunday before New Year's, we took a big step by agreeing to film our marriage testimony so the church could put together a short video to present before the sermon. We didn't specifically mention the affair in the testimony, but we did share how we were very close to separating and that God had given us the verse of Isaiah 43:19.

Though we had been through a lot of healing, there were still lots of emotional ups and downs. In that prior year, there was a move, a confession, a new normal, a new church, new friends, new jobs, a new school, a bankruptcy, and giving up homeschooling the kids.

My life goals, whether spoken or not, shifted. My life goal had been to have a marriage untouched by infidelity. I also planned to be a stay-at-home mom who homeschooled. My children were in school, and I was to become a working woman. It was a lot for me to take in.

Busyness helped to distract me and emotionally held me together for a while, but then, on other nights, I would sink into such depression that I would cry uncontrollably.

One night, I was inconsolable. Kenny tried to comfort and talk to me. I was curled up in a fetal position on our bed and just felt so utterly empty, sobbing my eyes out. He pulled me on the floor beside him and said, "Talk to Him. Just let it out. Tell Him what you're thinking and feeling."

Finding words was difficult, but I was brutally honest before God and Kenny and poured out all my burdens to God then. We also listened to worship music in our bedroom when I got like this.

For the first few months, I hardly cried at all. I just couldn't, and then when the tears finally started, it felt like they would never stop. I knew we had come far and felt secure in us. We had bonded considerably and were starting to make strides to develop our romance again. I fell in love with him, again.

I had learned love is a choice, after the betrayal, but having the emotions accompanied by that was nice. However, our marriage still was not where I wanted it to be. Yet. And that was the hard part for me. The waiting. The pain that still existed. The process.

I found great comfort in true stories of people who had been through the same thing whom God had restored and healed.

A friend of mine sent me a YouTube video of a couple who had been through an affair. In this case, it was the wife who cheated. The story was truly inspiring. The husband wanted to shame her and expose her, but through godly counsel, he chose to cover his wife with the love of God and embrace and protect her. Even more impressive was that the husband decided to love and accept the baby boy she had from the affair as his son—a wonderful, redemptive story.

I watched several videos, and there were periods of time between them. But this struck me: the guy still cried every time he told the story.

Sixteen years later, you could see the comfort, playfulness, and love between them on stage. But there were still tears.

I wanted to ask, "When do the tears stop?" I didn't want to be crying years later!

Perhaps what I thought were terrible tears weren't. At the time, my tears felt bad. Why? Because they came from pain, insecurity, doubts, fear of the future, and feeling inadequate.

The most tremendous grief to me, though, was the death of my dream—the death of a faithful relationship. I wanted a marriage untouched by infidelity. I wanted to be the only sexual partner my husband ever had. I wanted my knight in shining armor to forsake all others and cling to me, making me feel like the prized princess.

One Sunday morning in late January 2018, I was feeling very emotional. I missed Kenny, who had been on duty for several days. He came home that morning, and I felt needy and wanted extra confirmation from him.

I knew what I was doing. I was looking for him to fill the emptiness in my heart when I needed to seek God.

We took separate cars to church, and he went ahead with the kids. I went upstairs, so overwhelmed with emotion that I collapsed on the floor and had an ugly cry. So much of the hurt resurfaced, and grief over my dead dream.

Praying and staring at the woods outside my bedroom window, I wanted to melt into the scenery.

"God, I wish my heart was like nature outside, calm and still and showing Your glory." I didn't want to feel; I wanted to be strong, like a tree standing in the woods.

Gathering myself and my emotions, I headed to church despite being late. I missed the worship and caught the middle of the sermon. After service, I went to get prayer from a friend. We socialized in the fellowship hall while the second service began. I was ready to head home.

He asked me if I wanted to slip into the back of the sanctuary to catch the worship. They were about to do their last song. I was still feeling depleted and depressed and just wanted to go home. But I reluctantly agreed to it since I'd missed the first service worship.

During the final song, my emotions came crashing in again. The feelings were so intense that I couldn't even sing; I just cried.

One of our pastors, Christina, came up to the stage after the song and said she had a word to share that God had laid on her heart.

"I feel like someone here has experienced the death of something in 2017. The death of a dream, relationship, or something, and that the stench of it even now is very strong."

My heart was alert. God had my attention and was speaking directly to me again. *Oh, did this dream ever feel like death? And stench? Oh yes, hadn't I cried my eyes out only an hour ago?*

She continued, "I can't help but think of the story of Lazarus and how sometimes things have to die to become better, but God is bringing new life to this dream or relationship."

There it was again. God kept confirming He was making things new.

"Behold, I am doing a new thing; now it springs forth, do you not perceive it? I will make a way in the wilderness and rivers in the desert." Isaiah 43:19 (English Standard Version)

At home, I picked up my Bible and read the story. Jesus said that Lazarus' sickness wouldn't end in death. Lazarus did die, but Jesus raised him.

What's important is that he didn't stay down. And God used Lazarus' death to show His glory by raising him.

Jesus asked Martha if she believed He was the Resurrection and the Life. She did, but then she doubted when he asked for the stone to be removed.

Jesus said to her, "Didn't I tell you that if you believed, you would see the glory of God?" (John 11:40 Holman Christian Standard Bible)

That hit me. God's glory would be seen in my marriage, and He would breathe new life into it, but I had to stop doubting and believe. When I doubted, we would ever get to that place, I wasn't trusting God with my marriage.

I also thought more about the couple from YouTube and their tears. Maybe the tears they shed were not of fear, doubt, and fresh pain of betrayal but of thankfulness for God's faithfulness—tears of remembering how far he had brought them and what he had blessed and restored in their marriage.

If those were the kind of tears I would cry years from now, then I thought I would be okay with that.

Growing up, I came from a household where we regularly wrestled with each other. There were many tickling wars, piggyback rides, stealing my dad's socks off his feet, and hanging on dad's legs to try and bring him down during a wrestling match. Later, in my teens, my brother and I took karate and spared together.

After getting married, sometimes frustration or sexual energy was turned into wrestling matches. Even though Kenny always managed to pin me, those brief moments that I could get him for a second and tickle him mercilessly or get out of a hold kept me going. There has always been a restlessness or pent-up frustration/aggression in me that needed to come out occasionally.

That month, I'd been significantly restless. Dealing with a very tight budget, needing to downsize, beginning lots of part-time work, shifting my focus from being a homeschool mom to a working woman, and still adjusting to the new relationship with Kenny since the affair had left me stressed, depressed, and anxious.

One afternoon, my husband and I got into several wrestling matches. I felt like I had this pent-up frustration to get out. As I was getting ready for bed and thinking about wrestling, the story of Jacob wrestling with God came to my mind.

I went back to read the passage. "Then Jacob prayed, "God of my grandfather Abraham and God of my father Isaac, hear me! You told me, Lord, to go back to my land and to my relatives, and you would make everything go well for me. I am not worth all the kindness and faithfulness that you have shown me, your servant. I crossed the Jordan with nothing but a walking stick, and now I have come back with these two groups. Save me, I pray, from my brother Esau. I am afraid—afraid that he is coming to attack us and destroy us all, even the women and children. Remember that you promised to make everything go well for me and to give me more descendants than anyone could count, as many as the grains of sand along the seashore." Genesis 32:9-12 (Good News Translation).

Jacob then sent gifts ahead to his brother and made his family come last behind the whole company of workers and people in his tribe, hoping they would get away if the first group was attacked.

…"he stayed behind, alone. Then a man came and wrestled with him until just before daybreak. When the man saw that he was not winning the struggle, he hit Jacob on the hip, and it was thrown out of joint. The man said, "Let me go; daylight is coming." "I won't unless you bless me," Jacob answered. "What is your name?" the man asked. "Jacob," he answered. The man said, "Your name will no longer be Jacob. You have struggled with God and with men, and you have won; so your name will be Israel." Jacob said, "Now tell me your name." But he answered, "Why do you want to know my name?" Then he blessed Jacob. Jacob said, "I have seen God face-to-face, and I am still alive"; so he named the place Peniel. The sun rose as Jacob was leaving Peniel, and he was limping because of his hip."

Genesis 32:24-31 (Good News Translation)

Several things struck me. Jacob was reminding God of His promises to prosper him and thanking God for all He'd done. But Jacob openly admitted he was afraid to face his brother. He sent his family on ahead and then wrestled with God in the form of a fleshly opponent.

So, it seems he was wrestling with fear and not wanting to face uncertainty, but was he also wrestling to trust God and His promise? God told him he would prosper him; God said He would be with Jacob wherever he went…

"Remember, I will be with you and protect you wherever you go, and I will bring you back to this land. I will not leave you until I have done all that I have promised you."

Genesis 28:15 (Good News Translation)

After having his hip dislocated, he was still hanging on, refusing to let his opponent go until He blessed him.

I love that people in the Bible are like us: imperfect, messed up, and weak at times. Like me, I thought Jacob needed another reminder or confirmation that God was with him and would preserve and prosper him. And God did bless him.

Was his struggle real? Yes, and it turned out to be painful as well. It left a mark on Jacob that he carried for the rest of his life: a limp. But it was a struggle that made him stronger.

In my own life, I still wrestled with the dreams I had for my marriage. This was not the plan I had. And there were still lessons, healing, and fears I had to wrestle through in that process.

Just like Jacob, I wanted to know… God, will you bless me for staying, forgiving, and restoring? Will you make my marriage new as you promised? Will you provide for me? Will you be with me no matter what happens or how my life turns out?

What I love about the end of the wrestling match is that the sun rose over him as Jacob walked ahead to face his fears. It seems possible that the purpose of stating that in the text is to symbolize God's love and favor over him.

And the actual meeting with his brother couldn't have turned out any better! Esau embraced his brother, and there was grace and peace between them. This big giant of Jacob's was transformed into a miracle meeting.

Though I knew there were still battles to overcome, this Bible lesson encouraged me to keep moving forward.

In February 2018, our church was launching a Freedom Group study. This study would last nine weeks and finish with a big weekend conference.

There was something extraordinary about our small group that met in Myrna's home and was led by Priscylla and her husband Gustavo. Our Freedom group consisted of four other couples and one of the guys who had been in Kenny's men's group.

From the first meeting, I could tell this would be a unique experience. The group's openness and honesty seemed to come from nowhere, especially for people who didn't know each other well. We all dove in headfirst and wore our hearts on our sleeves.

Each week, a different person in the group was put in "the hot seat." This was just a chair in the middle of the living room. We all gathered around that person and prayed specifically for them.

The week I volunteered to go to "the hot seat," I was still feeling the heaviness of depression, grief, stress over finances, work, and unstable emotions over our marriage.

Some people knew our story, but the others didn't. I shared with those who didn't know and asked for prayer over continued healing in our marriage.

The room grew quiet as they waited for the Holy Spirit to lay on their hearts how to pray. Each one had a vision they felt led to share with me.

Valerie said she saw a flower in a field (representing me) being showered with God's love and blessings, but it wasn't because of anything I had to do to earn it. I just needed to let Him pour His blessings down. She said to know that God loves me, not the wife, mother, and homeschool teacher, but April—just who I am.

Priscylla said she saw a dry tree. A sad, poor-looking tree. But the tree had deep roots that would turn green again and flourish.

"Don't look back," she said. "Don't ask what if things had been different. You need to look ahead."

Manny saw a big metal boat carrying heavy cargo. It felt heavy and burdensome. He asked if I would rather be the big solid ship or a light sailboat tossed in a big storm?

He said, "The heavy cargo is precious. It is meant to help someone else." Those words were encouraging. I wanted to know that God would use these trials and that God could help someone else with our story.

Myrna saw a picture of a bucket of water that would be poured out for washing. Though it might be painful, it was a gentle washing of my life.

Rick said he thought of the story of Peter walking on the water to Jesus. He said that if I looked back or down, I would sink, and I had to keep my eyes on Jesus. I knew that to be true. When I started to lose my focus on Jesus, I did feel like I was sinking.

Cher saw a beautiful flower open and full, then closed tightly in a bud. When it reopened, it changed entirely into a different flower. After reflecting on her vision, I felt that I could see how my life had been beautiful, but with the pain of the affair, I did curl up tightly in a bud. Over time, God had grown and healed me, and now my flower's beauty was different.

Gustavo saw Kenny and I standing together. My hands were cupped with ashes. He said he wondered why I didn't give my ashes to God. Then he said that I threw them up into the air, and the ashes became sparkles of gold. As soon as he mentioned this vision, I immediately thought of the verse God had comforted me with during the first week after Kenny's confession.

"I will make you like a threshing board,

with spikes that are new and sharp.

You will thresh mountains and destroy them;

hills will crumble into dust.

You will toss them in the air;

the wind will carry them off,

and they will be scattered by the storm.

Then you will be happy because I am your God;

you will praise me, the holy God of Israel." Isaiah 41:15-16 (Good News Translation)

Gustavo didn't know that verse had meaning to me. His vision was a reminder of what God had promised.

Later that week, I met Diana for lunch. I told her about the affair a few months earlier. Diana surprised me by sharing that her first husband had pretended to be someone he was not, and he had also been unfaithful.

"I've been thinking about your question to me about how I got over my previous marriage and his unfaithfulness. I don't remember the pain. When I think about it, it was like it was someone else's life."

She continued, "God fully healed me. I believe God will do the same thing for you. And it will be as if it never happened. Just like a scar, you could touch it but would no longer feel its pain. And it won't reopen because it is healed."

I was listening carefully as she said these things to me.

"I believe you will embrace (Taylor) one day, and you will not feel insecure or inferior to her anymore." Those words shocked me.

"That's hard to imagine or believe ever happening right now," I replied.

"I think God will do that in your heart. And don't worry that Kenny had sex with someone else. It doesn't break or change your bond. What God brought together man cannot separate." Diana said.

She knew I had insecurities because of the affair and that the sexual piece was challenging for me to come through.

The week before, I had an opportunity for my blog to reach many more people. A woman who was more of a mainstream blogger invited me to write a piece to be featured on her blog. This was very exciting as I saw the traffic on my site increase due to a link from her blog to mine. The topic I wrote on was "Sexual Intimacy After An Affair."

I knew Kenny and I still had a bond despite what had happened, but I felt the distance before the confession. I also felt Taylor's "ghost," so to speak, in our sex life afterward. I often had to fight battles to get her out of my mind and images of them together when we were intimate. In the guest blog post, I listed some things that helped us.

- "For a while, we kept the lights on. I wanted him to see me and know he was having sex with me. It made me feel more secure.

- Grieving together made a big difference in bonding and healing.

- Pray, pray, pray. God created sex. He, too, cares about our sexual intimacy and healing.

- Seeing my husband's repentance was huge in allowing me to open up to him and respond sexually to him.

- Outside of the bedroom, we needed to have some time together to date, do something fun, and bond together."

(https://forgivenwife.com/healing-husbands-affair/)

I saw people reading my blog worldwide—from India, Britain, Australia, China, and Africa. These are places I wouldn't have thought would have read an American blog. It was so interesting to me, though, that as specific as the blog was, there were people hurting and searching for answers worldwide. My most popular posts were on making the decision to stay or leave, processing anger, sexual intimacy, and cleaning up after the affair.

Your Journey, Your Story

Once the tears start, you may wonder if they'll ever stop. Just like anger, tears, and emotional sorrow can come in waves. Tears may seem like an inconvenience, but in the long run, they are a wonderful cleansing tool that enables you to grieve.

If we heal properly, later on, those tears won't hold the same pain they do now. You may be obsessing over the affair, constantly thinking about it. When will I stop thinking about this? When will this stop being my every thought, my every breath?

Hang in there. It will begin to fade eventually. Something helpful to me during this time was activities that were engaging and fun.

I remember taking an exercise instructor training class. My mind was occupied enough that I was only able to think about the affair a few times during the day rather than every few minutes! It was a massive relief to have that break.

Try to find some projects that you can work on that require you to focus. Consider ice skating, a class of some sort, volunteering, sports, arts, or anything that will refresh you and give you some distraction.

Diana's on Christmas Eve. Diana, April, Caleb & Allie

Girls from my Freedom Group. This was taken at a Murder Mystery Party. April, Priscylla, Valerie, Myrna

7

Freedom

Freedom Group continued each week; finally, it was Kenny's turn to be in "the hot seat."

Kenny embraced Jesus fully after the confession, but he had been so convinced he was beyond grace and not chosen by God. After reading the Breaking Free devotional, he'd felt a sliver of hope that maybe he was a child of God after all.

With the truth out and his heart committed to repentance, he still cried over the gift of grace he had been given and the love he felt from God. Because of the sexual sin in his life early on, he always felt distant from God and not worthy of His love.

Many had supported and encouraged us, but some seemed to judge and see the old Kenny, not the new one God was changing.

Kenny still struggled to feel confident in his identity as a child of God. So, we gathered around him, and Priscylla read from Psalms 19.

She said she felt that God wanted to revive Kenny and reassure him of the promises He had given him.

Gustavo stepped in, "The enemy has tried to steal your identity all throughout your life because he knows the plans God has for you and the great man of God that you are. And as we are speaking these words, I can see the enemy whispering in your ear saying, Oh, if only they knew. The Lord knows the true identity that He sees in you. He does not see what you see in the mirror. The enemy whispers in your ear day and night, saying you don't amount to anything or what you are doesn't matter. But it matters to God." He continued.

"Remember, the Bible says we were adopted into God's family. Adoption is a choice. Remember, when people adopt kids, they choose to. They choose to love. It was God's choice to choose us, to choose you. You were brought into this family of God because God sees in you, His Son. He looks at you and sees the Son. This Son that shines on you and warms you is restoring you.

The Bible says that Jesus is the Son of Righteousness and so I pray that your identity is in God's love. You are fruitful and a man of God. We are not saying perfection here. Because none of us are there. You are a son of the Living God, and He is saying that He is well pleased with you and with your heart because of Jesus who lives in you.

Don't look back and let your past define you or dictate your identity. Remember Lot's wife? She looked back and was frozen, paralyzed. If you look back and focus on mistakes and let them define you, it's going to paralyze you. And that's what the enemy wants, for you to turn into a statue that stays stuck in this season of life.

God wants you to move into something different. He wants you to move your marriage forward and your family forward to give you two a future of hope. That's what you have to speak into your life. Use the Word of God against those lies of the enemy."

The support we had from this group was phenomenal. It was truly a blessing to us as we continued to work on healing. The words of life they spoke and prayed over us, and the weekly encouragement kept us going.

However, the enemy was not interested in our freedom and healing. I struggled severely with depression the last several weeks leading up to the

Freedom Conference. I also had two bad dreams with Taylor in them, which I believe were Satanic attacks.

The first night I had one of those dreams, waking at three am. While Kenny slept, I laid my hand on him and prayed over us and our marriage.

Finally, Freedom Weekend was upon us. It started on a Friday night. Different topics and areas of strongholds were discussed. As each area was discussed, such as anger, we would go forward for prayer. The intercessor would pray over us, and we would confess and rebuke that stronghold from our lives.

During prayer time, worship music was played, and many volunteers were at the back of the church, just interceding and praying for all of us. They were praying for the Holy Spirit to work in our hearts, for chains to break, for healing to occur.

The presence of God was undeniably present. That weekend, the sanctuary was saturated with His presence. Tears were shed as many of us faced sins that had kept us captive for years.

Saturday morning, we returned for a full day of breaking chains. They separated the men from the women. Men were on one side of the church, and women on the other. I sat beside Kay and Valerie. The session began with soul ties. They described a soul tie as anything sexual that forms a bond with you other than your spouse; this could be mental or physical.

On the stage, they enacted an illustration of having sexual baggage and soul ties between a couple. This illustration was powerful for me as I knew there were many soul ties to Kenny from his past. The tears started to flow again, and Kay and Valerie silently rubbed my back, knowing how this illustration affected me.

All were given cards to write the names of any soul ties. I wrote my list and included Taylor's name as well. I went forward for prayer, asking forgiveness for the impure thoughts in my life that had created ties, and for power to break the bond that Taylor had made with him.

My prayer partner prayed over me and the list of names. She told me to tear the paper up and stomp on it when she was done. I did. It felt good to give it to God and let it go.

I wondered how Kenny was doing on the men's side of the room. The church was so big I couldn't see him.

I went to the conference knowing I had some work to do in pride and anger. But I didn't know how God would show me my heart in an unexpected area.

The session was about shame. *Check. I have no problems with this. I don't feel shame for anything.* I didn't have a "past" that would cause me to feel guilty and ashamed about my actions. But as they described how the stronghold of shame played out in a person's life, I started to see my familiar pattern.

Throughout my marriage, I always made excuses for my behavior. When I was in the wrong, or even if I at least played a part in doing wrong to my partner, I always struggled to admit fault or apologize. This went side by side with pride as well.

What was I risking admitting my sins? I was acknowledging shame.

It was easier to insist I was right and "cover" myself with the proverbial fig leaves of excuses and good works than admit I rightly should be ashamed of my sins.

I grew up with the head knowledge that salvation is only through Jesus. No matter how many good works I do, I cannot earn my way to heaven. However, that still never really got to my heart. I still felt God would love me more if I did more good things, and when I failed, He loved me less.

I'd lived like a Pharisee, believing that I still, in some way, had something to contribute to my salvation. I gave this to God at the conference. I was tired of living with this Pharisee mentality. I needed His grace because I couldn't cover my shame.

They invited me to be baptized later that day. Although I had been baptized at the age of twelve, this new surrender of my shame made me want to recommit again to the salvation of grace in Jesus Christ.

We took a lunch break and broke off with our church group. I finally reconnected with Kenny. His eyes were red from so much crying, but approaching me, he said,

"Those ties are all broken off."

We embraced. I told him how much the shame session had affected me and that I wanted to get baptized again. After understanding my reasons, he agreed.

Many people were baptized. When it was my turn, Priscylla was in the baptism tub waiting for me to climb in. We briefly talked. I cried as I told her I just wanted to claim Jesus' righteousness and not my own. That it was all Him, I didn't deserve God's forgiveness, but I accepted it by grace. I went into the water and was pulled back up, humbled.

It was a powerful weekend for us and played a massive role in our marriage and healing journey. Living in freedom is still a process. We were freed from many things, but there is continued work to be done to claim the word of God and His promises in all things.

Our anniversary was approaching. The year before had been so fresh after the confession that I had no desire to celebrate. I was still battling conflicting emotions over this upcoming anniversary.

I originally wanted to renew our vows and have a small ceremony and celebration with friends, but now I didn't feel like doing that. My emotions rode a rollercoaster of ups and downs.

I booked an Air B & B camper in northern Virginia. The piece of property where the camper was situated was beautiful. As we explored the area, we followed the country road that wound past an old Civil War mansion, a horse carriage house, and an ice shed. Following tractor tracks, we wandered into the farmer's field late that afternoon. There was a beautiful view of the mountains around us, with the setting sun turning the wheat fields golden. I snapped many pictures and delighted in the soft summer breeze. We returned to the camper to cook dinner on the grill.

Later, we tried to start a fire, but the wood in the firepit was too damp. So, we sat around our fireless pit as I played worship songs on my guitar.

We discussed what had changed and what we'd learned about our marriage in the past year. The following day, we did some sightseeing before returning home.

A week later, while searching through Facebook messages for a friend's conversation, I unexpectedly came across an old thread from Taylor. As I reread it, I noted the dates on the messages, realizing that she had reached out to me three days after the affair started. Her message simply said, "I miss you." *Why?*

How could she? Why had she tried to keep a relationship with me like nothing happened? This triggered old emotions.

We squeezed our family vacation into the last week of summer 2018. Choosing to camp, our gear packed the Jeep so full that the kids had to hold things on their laps. There was no spare room for groceries.

Kenny and the kids worked on unpacking and setting up the campsite while I went shopping for food. Upon my return, Kenny showed me what he had done to our tent.

A bohemian-style cover decorated our air mattress. Little foldable tables conveniently stood beside the mattress. And a big colorful sheet hung in our tent for decoration and privacy. Outdoors, a string of white lights, and an ornate lantern cast a beautiful design from the decorative grating. He added atmosphere and glam to the camp.

When the kids went to bed each night, I got to pick a different pair of lingerie panties. He put a lot of time and effort into romancing me on this trip.

Your Journey, Your Story

"Two people are better off than one, for they can help each other succeed. If one person falls, the other can reach out and help. But someone who falls alone is in real trouble."

Ecclesiastes 4:9-10 (New Living Translation)

Popular movies like Superman or Batman often portray the hero saving the day by flying solo. This is not an act I recommend following.

We were not meant to do life alone. Left to our own thoughts and fears, we can feel isolated and overwhelmed.

Godly friendships, church, family, and counseling deeply impacted our journey.

Professional counseling is important for processing and healing work. Having a close friend, pastor, older mentor, prayer partner, or support group is invaluable.

You are about to get in the ring to fight. You are fighting to heal, understand, survive, save your marriage, or begin again.

When boxers get in the ring, they can get worn down. They need a coach to help them block the punches and learn strategies and a crew to rub their shoulders while encouraging them to get back in the ring.

Is your spouse willing to go to counseling with you? Even if not, you will benefit from talking with someone who is trained in affair recovery.

Whether you choose to stay with your spouse or not, many things need to be processed with the help of a godly counselor to heal effectively, regardless of what your spouse does.

Have you reached out to anyone for support? Is there at least one person you can trust to confide in? Do you have godly people who can pray over you and give you Biblical wisdom?

In the illustration of the ring, what are you fighting for the hardest right now? What verse is your fighting verse? The one that encourages you to keep going?

Baptism at Freedom Conference. Priscylla, April

Our Anniversary getaway, exploring the countryside.

April & Kenny

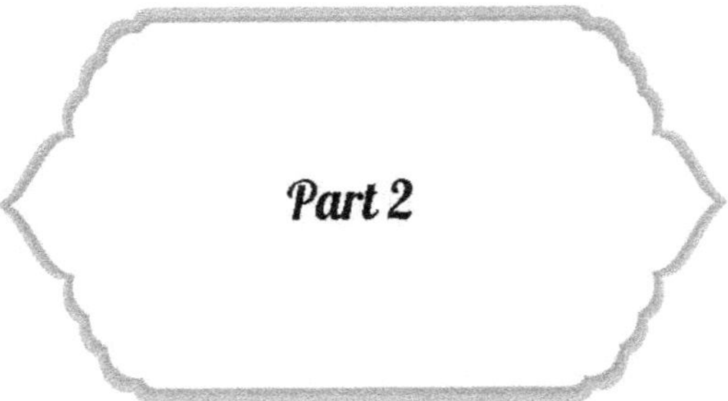
Part 2

8

The Crack

In the fall of 2018, Kenny had a hectic work life. In addition to his full-time paramedic job with the government, he also worked at an ER. I, on the other hand, had been juggling working at two different gyms and cleaning houses until I landed a full-time job in personal property taxes. I was exhausted from working multiple jobs and taking on various responsibilities. Even though I didn't really want that kind of work, I accepted the opportunity to work for the county for financial reasons and security. I began learning all about personal property taxes. It was more in-depth than anything I had ever tried to learn and practice. It took me out of my comfort zone in so many ways. Though I applied myself to learning the job, I also tried to find ways to express my creativity and have an outlet at work for my interests.

I looked up goofy holidays to celebrate, such as Learn the Meaning of Your Name Day. I wrote each coworker's name on a card and the definition of their name. This was new to many of them, who never knew what their names meant. Little projects like this kept me going at work. However, inside, I felt like I was dying.

At night, I came home to drown out my stress and unhappiness with alcohol. I struggled with depression and purpose during that whole year. I lost touch with the friendships I'd had at church. Now working full time, I didn't have the same time to invest in my friendships. I focused so much on what I didn't have and wasn't happy about in our marriage.

Kenny felt alone spiritually, seeing the shift in me spiritually and emotionally. I was blown back and forth by whatever emotion I was hanging onto instead of pressing hard into God and grounding myself in His Word. I numbed the pain with distractions and alcohol.

Everything we had done to build our marriage, I now doubted. Ungratefulness dominated my attitude towards my spouse.

God was still working on me. I wasn't cooperating much, but that didn't stop Him. He was preparing me to surrender the things I needed to give Him once and for all. God was about to show me how impossible it was to change myself without His help and that my life would fall apart without Him.

The events that led to our separation started with a simple argument in the parking lot of a hospital. Our son had a severe injury and was transported by ambulance to the best orthopedic surgeons in Richmond, Virginia, in February 2020. However, the breakdown of our newly restored marriage had actually begun earlier than that, through small decisions, words, and doubts about God's promise that I struggled with. Looking back, I'd gotten lazy spiritually and dealt with depression and stress in the county job I held from October 2018 to 2019. In the summer of 2019, I still struggled to like my spouse. I loved him but focused on the negative things I disliked about him, which consumed me.

On the way to our family vacation that summer, I was in a foul mood. How he was so talkative that day annoyed me; he took too long to look up directions to get there, which was grating on my nerves.

I prayed against my negative feelings and thought my silence was adequate as I tried to hide my annoyance, but he could tell I was ornery. Unfortunately, my moodiness rubbed off on him. By the next day, though my mood had lifted, his began.

We spent the day at a lake divided. I stayed with the older kids in the deep water since there were no lifeguards, while Kenny stayed with our youngest, who played on the sandy beach. That evening, I felt like taking a walk. Our tiny Air B and B had little privacy. The kids slept in the only bedroom while we used an air mattress in the living room. Wanting a break after being on the water all day with the boys, I slipped my shoes on.

Frustrated and feeling abandoned, Kenny threw a wrench in my plans.

"Going on a walk? Why don't you take the kids?" Hearing the sarcasm in his tone, I returned an icy silence and took the kids with me.

As we wandered on trails around the area, bitterness, selfish desires, negative thoughts, and mindsets swirled around me with every step.

After the walk, I let them go inside while I stayed outdoors, breathing out frustration.

"Is this ever going to work? Is this really what I want? How is God making us new?"

I felt hopeless. More than anything, I felt the weight of my inability to change.

How could we survive if I didn't change? He had changed since the confession. Why couldn't I overlook our differences? Why was it the world's end when he did things slower or more methodically when I preferred plowing through it like a bull? Why couldn't I value the way he saw the world? Why did I have to judge his perspective and think the way I saw it was the only way?

Maybe I didn't want to fight for this marriage because it would require me to face my sins and deal with them.

Waiting in the darkness outside, I tried to pray, but I had already accepted defeat.

The door creaked as the dark living room enveloped me. He sat hard-faced on the small, flowered couch. I had been gone so long that the kids were already in bed. I sank beside him. We sat silently, the tension so thick you could cut it with a knife.

Recklessly, I began, "I don't think this is going to work. We are too different. I've failed to be the wife you deserve. I feel like I'm just biding my time until you grow unhappy enough to cheat again. You and Taylor have so much more in common. You would be better off going back to her or finding someone else." I finally paused after my vomit of words, waiting in the silence.

I saw him as an unfeeling villain, as my enemy. Yet, in the pause, his tears fell.

I had mocked everything we had tried to heal and rebuild. I'd told him to return to her when he left her and risked everything to fix us! Why had I done this? I loved myself and my sins and didn't want to love this person who was different from me.

I felt remorse. He wept bitterly, utterly broken. How could I bring him such grief? My tears fell, too. What a mess I was making. Holding him, I apologized and tried to comfort him.

The following day, our family took a 5-hour hike. He was still distant and hurting from the night before, but I thought we were okay after my apology. He hardly spoke a word the entire hike.

Later that night, we talked again. He said he had been trying to think all day about how we could make things work with a divorce or separation. Taken aback, I apologized again, telling him I'd been venting and didn't want to separate. He'd been burdened the entire day, carrying the weight of my words and thinking that was the direction I wanted us to go.

I wish I could say the rest of the vacation was fantastic, but it wasn't. It took him a lot of time to get over that hurtful conversation, and it set us back considerably in having a healthier marriage.

That was the first big crack that spread and broke our resolve in God's promise. We went through ups and downs. I felt distant from him. As time passed, our jobs and busyness continued to chip away at our relationship as neither of us was fully invested in building our marriage.

I noticed a piece of my engagement diamond was missing during this timeframe. There had been a crack, and now a tiny piece had fallen out of the setting. It was just a visible sign that our marriage was crumbling.

Back to my son's injury. I had been emotionally missing Kenny and kept pressing to have time with him. I could feel the distance and tried fixing what was already broken. During a nap after church that day, I dozed while he worked beside me in bed on an assignment from his college class.

Our younger son burst into the house to tell us our oldest had fallen from a tree and was hurting badly. After a bike stunt of riding under tree branches and grabbing hold of the overhead limb, he planned to let the bike go as he swung around the limb to land a jump. However, my oldest son didn't land the jump on his feet. He fell on his right arm, it was not broken through the skin, but it was hanging unsupported within the skin.

He held his arm as we walked and got into the car to go to the hospital. After seeing his x-rays, the doctor wanted him transported to Richmond's VCU. With the other kids at home, one of us would stay with our oldest and one with the other kids. I went home to pack an overnight bag for Kenny, who volunteered to go to VCU with our oldest.

After returning to the hospital parking lot to give Ken the bag, I commented that I had felt something would keep us apart that day. He bristled at those words.

I tried to explain. I wasn't trying to make light of the situation or our concerns for our son. I just missed him and knew we'd be separated again, as he had just worked seventy-two hours the night before. We hugged, and I thought that he understood me.

The next day, I met Kenny in the hospital waiting room. Surgery had already begun, and we were anxious to hear how things were going.

The doctor came out to tell us that although this was an incredibly unusual break for a young child, he was able to piece the bone back together and had put in wire, screws, and a rod to hold the arm together. They hoped he would regain nerve feeling and movement in his hand. The doctor's words were encouraging.

He left us, and Kenny asked if I had something to say about the other day. I was utterly confused as to what we had unfinished. We took our conversation to the hall, and he felt I was ungrateful for the time he had made to be with me. My comment in the parking lot sounded to him like complaining. It also made him feel defeated as he could never do enough to make me happy, a theme I had conveyed through negative, discontented words over many things in the past.

I cried in the hall and tried to explain that this was not my heart in this situation. I thought I was helping him and trying to share the burden by packing and bringing the overnight bag, but all I was trying to convey was that I missed him and wanted to be with him. He softened some, but as he pulled me in for a hug, I pulled back and became hurt and angry.

When called back into the recovery room, I was filled with shame. My tears fell silently, not for my son, but for my marriage. The doctors and nurses tried to reassure me, attributing my emotions to parental concern. However, I was nursing my emotional wounds and feeling even more distant from my spouse. I still felt the profound difference and invisible separation between us.

Later that February, we had a painful conversation. Kenny was quiet, withdrawn, cold, and emotionless toward me.

"I've lost hope in us." My heart froze. What do you mean? It's okay, Babe. We'll get through this." I tried to be encouraging and bring him out of this hopeless talk.

"I've read your diaries." *My diaries?* The blood drained from my face.

"You've always struggled to love me and feel happy with us. Even when we were dating."

I'd never hidden my diaries from him, yet I never imagined him pouring through them either. It was true that my feelings of love and happiness over our marriage did not come easily, and I had doubted many times.

"Kenny, a lot of what I wrote are moments of venting and processing feelings. I love you and am committed to you. Babe, I can make things better. I'm committed to changing. I've been thinking about getting some focused prayer time with God to tackle these changes that need to take place. Would you be okay with me going away one upcoming weekend for personal spiritual reflection?"

"Yes, that's okay. That might be best for you anyway, maybe God is trying to prepare you."

His meaning was implied. He wanted out. "I don't think we were meant to be together."

This was so opposite of how he always talked about us. He'd always encouraged our marriage, saying we were made for each other. I knew something was very wrong. My marriage was in crisis at this point. The next day, I sent a text message to a handful of friends.

February 26th, 2020

Girls, I am going out on a limb here, but I really need prayer. Kenny and I have had several conversations over the past month, and last night, we had a crushing discussion, leaving us both feeling hopeless and that we're coming to the end of our marriage.

There are far too many things to dish out and years of history and hurts. Besides the affair, I believe this is ultimately about my inability to change and like and look at him as a friend. I'm ashamed of this and distraught that after 16 years of marriage, I still cannot seem to fully appreciate or love him as I should.

He is worn down and broken. Please pray for the Holy Spirit to move and make a major change in my heart towards him and life in general. He sees my line of consistent negativity and unhappiness in life, mainly focusing on him as my scapegoat.

I don't mean to live like this, but it is a habit that seems impossible to break. If you are willing to be accountability partners for me, I think that is what I'm going to need...

Girls, I feel like I'm drowning, and I don't see a way out unless God miraculously changes me.

I called work, claiming a family emergency, because I wanted to spend the day with Kenny, trying to prove to him that he was a priority.

A few days later, a friend from church invited me to a worship night. I sought one of my friends out for prayer. She'd already spoken life and prayer specifically over our marriage during Freedom Group.

I don't remember all that Myrna prayed for, but with tears in her eyes, she said,

"April, I see your marriage, and it may look like embers that are growing cold, but I believe God's going to cause these embers to burn like a roaring fire again, a new fire."

March 10th, 2020

"Friends, it is late. I'm sorry. We have had another deeply painful conversation. Kenny's heart is closed. He is not being unkind, but unless God works a miracle in our marriage, Kenny is ready to end it.

Please pray and plead with me God would speak to us both, to confirm and establish His will and way in this situation."

He leaned against the pillows, blank-faced, unmovable, and unengaged. The painful conversation came to an end. Bowing my head on our bed, I started crying and praying in great agony. There were no words at this point. My heart was bleeding out.

Wordless sounds came from my mouth in groans and gibberish. It was purely from a heart crying out to God from the depths of my pain and anguish. I had no idea what to pray for. I needed God at that moment and felt His presence over me regardless of being speechless.

"I can't do this anymore," he said, walking to the shower.

The cadence of endless droplets fell as I lay restless on the bed. What should I do? I went downstairs and started to fold the laundry.

Determined to stick with my decision to change my behavior, I folded his clothes and continued serving him. Coming downstairs, he found me folding.

"What are you doing? You don't need to do that for me."

In his mind, we were through, so what was my purpose in helping him?

I looked at him and said, "As long as you are in my house, I will serve you."

We both teared up and held each other.

Your Journey, Your Story

One of the first questions asked after an affair is why? Asking this question can be hard; however, it can also be very enlightening for the spouse who was cheated on.

There is often a message in the affair—a reason why the spouse strayed. Each spouse contributes to the marriage. We cannot control our partner's actions or responsibilities, but we can control ours.

Are we willing to acknowledge our part in the marriage and the unhealthy things we contributed? If we want to repair the marriage after the affair, we will need help identifying what was broken in the relationship to fix it.

Were there things missing in the marriage? What did the affair partner provide for your spouse which was lacking in your marriage? Was your spouse trying to communicate their needs to you? Did you recognize those needs? Did you ignore them?

In my situation, it was not just a sexual situation. It was my spouse's need for emotional intimacy. I often strayed away from emotional intimacy. My spouse found that in this partner. I also was very critical of my spouse. And the affair partner affirmed him.

What was the atmosphere of the marriage? What did we contribute to the marriage that made it unhealthy or might have encouraged infidelity? Pray for a humble heart that is willing to allow God to show you areas in your life that need work.

Our hike to a mountain peak the day after I hurt him with my words.

9

Child of God

I drove to the mountains of Virginia and hiked to a waterfall before heading to my Air B and B for the night. Parking in the driveway of the historic house, I walked to the door and knocked. It appeared my host wasn't home.

I explored the grounds with an unusual wrought iron pagoda, horses, chickens, and statues.

Ding. Glancing at my cell, the host informed me she was running an errand and to make myself at home. Stepping inside, I traveled back in time. Antiques, hardwood floors, grand piano, built-in bookshelves, vintage lamps, and portraits reminded me of Downton Abbey. The old wooden staircase groaned. I went to my room on the second floor and locked myself in for the night. The spacious bed was piled with pillows.

Opening the wooden shutters, I sat on the chaise by the window. I texted Kenny. I tried to apologize for the past and be encouraging.

His return text revealed years of pent-up anger. I was defenseless against the jabs.

Trying not to defend myself, I accepted the words and offered my apologies.

Do not respond with a jab. You have chosen to plant good.

"Let us not become weary in doing good, for at the proper time we will reap a harvest if we do not give up." Galatians 6:9 (NIV)

God reminded me of this Scripture. I'd planted so much negativity with my words, expectations, and selfishness; now I was reaping what I'd sown.

Desperately, I sought to reverse the damage, clinging to God with all I had.

That night, lying in a strange bed, I read my Bible, prayed, listened to worship music, and cried. I felt so utterly alone. My only hope was in God. The scripture I clung to at this time was:

"I keep a grip on hope: God's loyal love couldn't have run out, His merciful love couldn't have dried up. They're created new every morning. How great your faithfulness! I'm sticking with God. (I say it over and over). He's all I've got left... When life is heavy and hard to take…Enter the silence. Bow in Prayer. Don't ask questions: Wait for hope to appear. Don't run from trouble. Take it full-face. The "worst" is never the worst. Why? Because the Master won't ever walk out and fail to return."

Lamentations 3:21,22-32 (The Message)

Listening to the pelting rain and snow outside the window made me thankful. Camping had been my plan. Frustrated that no campground around the area was available to book, I settled for the Air B and B. God had spared me from the miserable cold. Curling up in the warm bed I cuddled a life-size baby doll to my chest.

Though it was embarrassing to admit, the baby doll comforted me. It felt like a real infant was snuggled in my arms, and I could pretend someone loved and wanted me.

I lay listening to the song "No Longer Slaves" by Bethel Music on repeat. Tucked in a strange bed in the mountains with the snow falling, I clung to the doll and let those words wash over me.

I probably listened to the song hundreds of times during that season. I let those words cover me. *I AM a child of God.* That was my identity and foundation amid the chaos.

After I returned from my overnight trip, Kenny and I spent a night or two together without the kids. I was hopeful, wishing to bond and have some positive connection. But he was still detached.

Holding each other one night, I pleaded with him to give me a chance to change. He looked at me sadly and said, "I'm sorry, Babe, but I just don't believe this time will be different. Besides, you've said many times before you couldn't change."

Still unwilling to give up, I begged him to hang on and let me show him. I also asked him several times to tell me if there was someone else. He told me no.

While I was at work the following day, Kenny texted to tell me he would take the kids on a camping trip for the remainder of Spring break. He picked them up early from grandma's house.

It felt like a blow. He wasn't content to hang out with me. He wanted the kids' company. In a sense, I felt they were replacing me in this situation. *He's running away.*

My first reaction was hurt. But I calmly texted back positively. I tried to look at the situation in a new way. The old me would have been offended, disappointed and angry. I knew my feelings of hurt now were based on the strained relationship and my insecurities. The truth is, it was wonderful that this dad wanted to spend time with his kids. I didn't want to be selfish and stand in the way of their trip when I couldn't leave my job.

I texted the next day, thanking him for being a good dad and investing in our children. He responded that they were all doing fine and having a blast.

I could feel the coldness in the wording as if they didn't miss me and things were better without me. It stung. But I knew the jab came from a place of bitterness and resentment over vacations when I complained or was disappointed in something. He didn't have to wonder if everything was to my liking or comfort. I felt he was envisioning family life without me.

The house felt lonely. I continued reading and meditating on scripture daily, even at work. Carrying the Word of God in my pockets on a card.

I lived in a mist, numbed some days, surviving minute to minute. My weight dropped.

Spending three days without my family in an empty house was sobering. I continued trying to stay busy doing things that were helpful to Kenny. I cleaned the house, knowing he liked it when it was nice and neat. I did laundry and worked on our budget. I kept my promise to be responsible for sharing the burden of our finances.

Restless, I pulled his backpack out of the closet and rummaged through the contents. My fingers brushed the small circular ornament.

I held it in my hand, my heart hurt. *His wedding band.* The discovery stung; however, I also accepted it. I'd taken my band off once, too, after he confessed to the affair. *I can forgive this.*

Continuing the search, I rifled through papers.

The world stopped. My heart beat faster, my eyes devouring the content with urgency.

My stomach turned.

There were papers I could not explain–a name I recognized. My mind whirled in panic. I was piecing it all together. This was the woman Kenny only mentioned a handful of times, but my spirit sensed something special about her. An admiration, attraction, or something.

Were they sleeping together? Was it too late? How much of an emotional connection had been formed?

Calling my best friend, I poured out my discovery and questions.

"Check his friend list on Facebook, maybe she's there," Melissa suggested.

Clicking on his profile, I couldn't see his friends list.

Heart sinking, "He blocked me!"

"He is friends with her, and she is beautiful," Melissa confirmed, pulling up his profile.

We'd agreed not to accept friends with the opposite sex on Facebook since the affair. He'd broken another boundary.

I made an emergency call to my counselor the next day, telling her what I discovered. During my conversation with the counselor, I was emotionally capsizing. I hardly remember having an experience like that where I was completely consumed with panic, my mind spinning out of control. Thankfully, her words helped me stabilize some and find my footing.

I called my aunt in Connecticut. She was the one who spoke wisdom and life to me after Kenny's confession. I needed her again. Scared and unsure of what to do, her calming words and prayerful presence gave me support.

I had to prepare for Kenny and the kids to come home. I said nothing to him about what I found. They stayed in a hotel on the last night of the trip. I texted my oldest to find out if Ken was with them or if he had left them alone in the hotel room for any length of time. My mind was whirling, and I was concerned that maybe something was going on between this woman and him, even with this trip. However, that had not been the case.

As they drove home, I steeled myself, trying to stay busy, praying, and rehearsing how to confront this. How would I react once the truth came out? Last time, I'd been angry and violent. I also didn't want to talk around the kids, so I planned to wait until after they went to bed.

This was the ultimate test for me in self-control. I was working on obeying God by planting words of life in my marriage. I'd been doing well. Now, I was getting kicked right in the gut. My old wound, I feared, was going to reopen. I need to act with dignity.

I watched the progress of their journey on my location-sharing app. They were close. I didn't have much time. I flew upstairs to our room and kneeled on the floor one more time to plead with God. I prayed that the truth would be revealed. I didn't want any more lies. I wanted the truth, even if it hurt.

Returning downstairs, I worked on the computer at the kitchen table. I heard the door. Bags, pillows, bikes, and camping equipment were put away. The kids greeted me and then dispersed in different directions.

I held my breath as his footsteps climbed the stairs to the kitchen. I greeted him, trying to remain calm and collected and not too eager. I asked about the trip, and he told me they had been horseback riding that morning.

The conversation took an unexpected turn. My birthday was tomorrow, and the following day was his. We always celebrated together with a date night or weekend getaway. Not this year; my birthday felt like it would be a day to endure living in this limbo hell of uncertainty.

"Do you want to go out on a date tomorrow for your birthday?" He asked. I remained calm on the outside, but my pulse quickened.

How should I respond to this? Go figure, after weeks of pouring out kindness and life-giving words, refusing to return jabs, serving him, and asking him to give me a chance; NOW he asks when I don't know what to believe and what's going on in his heart.

"I don't know," I responded coolly. Now, it was his turn to be confused. "I thought you said you wanted to start dating and getting to know each other again?"

"I did, but I don't know now. There's something I need to talk to you about later tonight when the kids are in bed." He grew quiet and serious yet remained seemingly confused. "I don't think I can wait. You need to tell me now."

"All right," I said, shutting my laptop. "Let's go upstairs."

My emotions and nerves started kicking in, overwhelmed, I took deep breaths. Blowing out slowly and trying to remain calm. Tears were coming, and it took everything to remain composed.

Shaking considerably at this point out of fear, anger, and anxiety, I spoke. "I want you to know I respect you and ask that you respect me. I want you to tell me the whole truth and not lie to me."

Sitting on the bed, I calmly laid the paper between us. "Can you explain this to me?"

Visible relief came over him. He shook his head in disbelief. "April, this is a joke. I found it online.

Shaking my head, "I wish I could believe that, but there's this," I said, pointing at her name with a wildly shaking hand. "Yes, yes, I know that was for a joke at work."

He claimed nothing was going on sexually between them. He admitted the joke was in bad taste.

I told him about being blocked on Facebook, about finding they were friends, and I asked if they were also texting and how far that had gone. He said he was not having another affair, that they were friends and texted but that was it.

Wisdom, however, was clearing the situation for me, and I disagreed. "You may not have gone as far this time as you did with Taylor, but you are breaking boundaries and are having an emotional affair, let alone taking steps into a sexual one. You don't just joke around sexually with someone you aren't attracted to or send pictures to them if you don't admire them."

Relieved that he seemed to be telling the truth and they weren't at a sexual stage, I said, ``I'm glad I know what's going on because now I know what I'm dealing with." He gave a sarcastic grunt at this.

I could feel his resistance. I felt hope because maybe this had been stopped soon enough; we could still fix our marriage and not go into more heartache. But after further conversation, it became apparent I was still on the firing end of the stick. I was in a vulnerable place. He was filled with hopelessness over us ever getting better, anger over years of buried hurts I'd caused. His heart was hardened. This wasn't going to be like last time. He was fully repentant and willing to do anything I asked to regain trust, establish boundaries, and fight for me four years earlier. But now he was bitter and closed, and I truly felt like I couldn't make rules or demands of him.

I asked him to stop being friends with her on Facebook and texting her. At the time, he said they hadn't written for a while anyway. We had a counseling session to discuss trying to separate for a while, feeling we needed a break to work on things but not in such close quarters.

We started sleeping separately at this point. He went to the couch downstairs while I stayed in our bedroom. I didn't want to fix us with sex. We had done that too many times before, always being drawn back together and fixed for a while, yet never truly correcting the root issues in our marriage.

Sensing his coldness and wavering commitment to our marriage, I struggled to give myself sexually to him, feeling unloved in many ways because I didn't feel safe or secure.

My birthday came. I awoke to a text from my bestie Melissa, perhaps one of the most meaningful messages I have ever received.

Good Morning, my dear friend. Happy birthday! I know it's a different kind of birthday for you, but I hope it's still lovely and that God shows you beautiful things just for you. I was up until after midnight, praying in your day. I was praying for the Holy Spirit to be in you like you've never known before. That this year you'd experience Him like you never have. I love you so much, and you're one of the best gifts God has ever given me.

I was knitting for a while last night, and the project I'm working on is a shawl in sunset colors. It made me think of all the many nights we sat under the stars, sharing our hearts, hopes, dreams, and heartbreaks. I couldn't help but smile in a way I haven't in a long time.

You are a treasure, and I am praying the Holy Spirit will reveal wonderful things to you today and over this new year of your life.

I had a very brief dream about you. You were moving a mountain, but it wasn't like the whole mountain just got out of the way. You were moving, with your hands, ridiculously large pieces of rock and dirt to a different place. It was slow, but effective.

This message meant so much to me. The love and friendship between us and the mention of her dream. We often laughed about the crazy dreams or nightmares she sometimes had. This was different.

This was precisely what I was doing with God's help. Slowly, yes, so slowly, but effectively, I was planting new life and changing.

A week later, I desperately reached out to my friends again for prayer by text

March 30th, 2020

Girls, I'm sorry I'm airing out my dirty laundry, but I'm sitting in darkness right now asking for a miracle. Kenny and I have decided to separate. There were hurts on both sides, and I feel like the work God needs to do in my heart needs to be done separately.

For one, being so controlling or dependent on Ken has been an issue, so I need to depend fully on God. I am gaining some serious spiritual strength. God is working powerfully through the scriptures to stabilize my mind and already seriously starting to change me.

I hesitate to share this because it's not the kind of thing you want known but another woman is involved again. When I found his wedding ring in his backpack and paperwork pointing to her, I confronted him. He admitted to flirting with her at work and texting. After that came out and we had a counseling session. I thought he was still willing to work on us and give her up.

I've been serving him, building him up with my words, and trying to be supportive. He just put money on a room that he can't move into till next *week, but it's right down the street from where they work. She is married but obviously unhappy too.*

Tonight, he was smiling and texting on his phone. I asked about it and he is still texting her. This is ripping my heart out. I really am trying to fight for us even though I know that means trying to gain trust again. He seems so double-minded right now. I don't know what to believe. All I know is he's resisting God and still trying to fix his heart with idols.

We had a fight and I poured out my heart. I kept asking him what he was doing! And tell him I'm willing to fight, and that I believe we can get through this. Claiming he is a child of God and to stop running! But I also told him I cannot share him with another woman, and I need him to make a decision. He needs to let her go or I am going to have to give up.

The questions and doubts will be rampant if he moves out. Please pray for him right now! I'm begging for a wall of prayer and the Holy Spirit to penetrate his heart. He's throwing us away and I can't stop him. I've never seen him just give up like this. I feel so utterly alone. Please pray God moves right now tonight.

That was the most painful night, as I sobbed hysterically on the carpet in my room. I pleaded with him to stop texting her. To stop throwing us away. I said anything to sway him and bring him back to his senses. Nothing moved him.

He sat with a vacant dull look in his eyes as I carried on emotionally frantic. No comforting words, no assurances, he was already gone in heart; his body just hadn't left yet. Now, as I lay in a fetal position, snot so thick I could hardly breathe, crying out to God, his footsteps outside the door stopped.

He reminded me to wash my hands because I had touched and held onto him. He was home in quarantine because of exposure to Covid. I felt angry and alone.

Why not just catch COVID and die? I don't care. He doesn't care about me anymore; I'm on my own.

Anger was taking over now. I felt bitterness and frustration over the choice he was making. There was no way to stop him.

I read about separation so I knew that until we had documentation of when the separation started, we couldn't get a divorce until we'd been separated for six to nine months.

A divorce was not what I wanted, but I also didn't want a separation to last longer if he was determined to divorce. I wanted it over and done if he was unmovable. So, I typed up a paragraph giving the date and circumstances as to why we chose to separate and a place we could sign.

The next morning, I handed it to him. He read and refused to sign it because his relationship with the coworker was mentioned.

"The way it's written implies infidelity. I'm not having an affair. I won't sign it. Take that part out."

Disgruntled, I erased it and kept the irreconcilable differences instead.

"Don't you think it's better this way?" He said, referring to the separation. "Isn't that what you've wanted for so long? You've never been happy with me anyway."

Pursing my lips, I shook my head. I wasn't going along with this. I didn't want this, but acceptance was bitterly setting in. I needed him out. Sleeping separately, we'd abstained from sex.

Knowing he seemed to have no commitment to me, I wanted space. This was far too painful. I dug up as much money as I could spare to help him get a room to rent somewhere quickly. Within a few days, he had found a room to rent in someone's house. He was packed up and gone.

The conversation with the kids seemed to go ok. We explained to our youngest that it was like two kids at a playground who had a disagreement and needed some time to be apart and have a timeout before playing together again.

Our youngest had some questions, but the older boys just took it silently, being aware that more was at stake.

We agreed that Kenny would come to help with the kids on days he wasn't on duty. Some nights, when I got home from work, he would stay and have dinner with us, if I invited him, but he would leave for the night.

He and I lost a lot of weight during this time, as the stress and depression made it hard to eat. We mutually hugged each other for some comfort, but it was always tentative, and we would ask permission from the other person.

I took the kids hiking one weekend since most things were shut down because of COVID-19. Some weekends, we had designated family time, but some outings I did not invite him to join us.

On one such outing, I took the kids to a new park we'd never been to before. When we got home, Ken had returned from a bike ride and was putting the bike back in our garage.

I held myself back in many ways at this time. I wasn't trying to be cruel but also wasn't gushing with sympathy either, just trying to be civil and hold him at arm's length.

The kids greeted him as I set our daypack down. He appeared sad and solemn. After the kids dispersed upstairs, he remained seated on the bottom steps.

Struggling for words, he glanced up, "I think I'm ok, but I feel like I need to let someone know that I got so depressed today I felt suicidal. I've never felt that strongly before. I just came into the house while you guys were gone and collapsed on the floor. I felt so hopeless like I needed to call someone until it finally passed."

I cared about him, but I also felt tough love, wisdom, and focus I didn't have before.

"I'm not surprised, Kenny. Where is your support? I have people around me helping to hold me together, and I'm seeking God. What are you doing?"

I calmly climbed the stairs, hoping my words would make him stop and think. The door closed, and I heard his car start up and leave.

Later, I couldn't see his location on Google Maps. Not knowing where he was and getting no response, I called his sister, requesting she reach out to him. I explained my concern he might be suicidal. Thankfully, nothing happened. The way he handled the separation was starkly different from how I was handling it. I was fully relying on God and feeling a deeper focus and peace than I had in a long time. Although I was more focused on finding comfort in God, it didn't make letting go of the life I wanted with my spouse any easier.

After he moved out, I needed our home to look different. His pictures and leftover belongings were painful reminders of what I'd lost. I gave our bedroom a makeover. I put away our pictures. In their place, I strung up a banner that said, His banner over you is love. I created a vision board with pictures of the children and scripture verses. Hanging a colorful canopy over my bed, I pinned the words, I am a child of God, to it so I could look up and be encouraged. Scripture verses went everywhere: on my walls, mirror, and kitchen cabinet fronts.

One morning, while I was preparing to leave for work, he came upstairs to talk with me before I headed out. Noticing the changes I'd made to our bedroom; he made some jabs.

"How do you like the single life? It looks like you moved on quickly, removing any trace of me from your life."

Angry, I felt like responding with a jab of my own, but I saw the comment for what it was. *He is insecure. Speak the truth. Let him know where you stand.*

"No, I do not enjoy single life. However, I can't have reminders of you everywhere if you don't want to be with me. This is survival."

He backed off at this reply. I wasn't playing games anymore. It was the truth. During this conversation, I asked about her and if he was still texting her. He did not deny it. I got angry and emotional. He tried to reach out and comfort me, but I coldly told him not to touch me and left the room.

Your Journey, Your Story

I went through an identity crisis when my spouse separated from me. I had been a wife. I had been a lover. I had been a mother, and now, this role of being a spouse and lover was no longer wanted.

I felt lost and struggled with my worth and struggled with who I was without my spouse.

People often introduce themselves by name and then follow with their job title. We often define ourselves by what we *do* instead of who we *are.*

Who we are should reflect the core of our beliefs and values, not feelings. But the secret to an unchanging identity is one grounded on an unshakable foundation. That identity is found in **Whose** we are.

When we accept and believe what God says about us, we can rest in that truth. If we are in a relationship with Jesus Christ, we are a child of God. That's an identity that will never change.

In Jesus Christ, we are sons and daughters of the King. I encourage you to search the scriptures for what God says about his people. We are loved. We are adopted. We are valuable in His sight.

Part of the identity crisis may come from years of marriage and the millions of thread connections made from being a part of each other.

When God designed marriage, two become one. When they are separated, there is a tearing.

If your spouse does not want to reconcile, don't let this defeat you. God can still fill in these pieces that will feel empty for a while. When that spouse leaves, you will develop. Your role may change as a wife, but your identity in Jesus will never change.

10

Rewrite

A shift was taking place. As I continued mentoring with my godly aunt, she greatly encouraged me to invest in the children. Kenny and I spent so many years focused on us and our marriage that the children had taken a backseat. Riding waves of issue after issue in our marriage, we would come together and patch the hole until another marital emergency arose. The kids became a side attraction or accessory rather than valued people to invest and pour into.

Changing my focus, I spent more time with them. We cooked, played games, watched movies, went canoeing, hiked, and talked together. Covid caused life to slow down in ways that helped our family bond, especially during the separation. My oldest was sensitive to me and would often ask if I was okay or offer a loving hug when I needed it most. I tried to assure the children that no matter what happened, we loved them, and God would never abandon them.

I got a text from Kenny one day telling me that an older Christian guy from the hospital he worked at had reached out to him. He had heard about our separation and was trying to mentor and be an accountability partner for Kenny. This man had also experienced brokenness in his marriage and was trying to encourage Kenny not to make the same mistakes he had.

I had been in prayer for a mentor for Kenny. His heart wasn't open to finding someone then, so it was a huge answer to prayer that this man was pursuing Kenny. God made provision from an unlikely source.

Family days continued with Kenny. Confined at home more than ever due to COVID-19 practices, we got creative with activities. Special meals, games, science projects, and silly-themed parties helped to pass the evenings.

Slowly, Kenny showed interest in me. As I pulled back and stopped pleading with him but just held my ground, he realized he wasn't ready to let go. However, he still seemed to be floating in limbo, not committed to me but not letting go of me either, unsure of what he wanted.

One night, he brought up a male Facebook friend of mine who had complimented one of my photos.

After the affair, I'd wiped 90% of male friends from my list. I had crossed no boundaries with this guy and respected his marriage, but Ken was hypersensitive and insecure with this comment from him. He felt like it was a double standard.

This was a heated conversation in which I talked down to him and wasn't as kind. I didn't feel he was playing fair. He was oversensitive to the weakness in himself. He asked me to please stop speaking disrespectfully to him.

I agreed to delete this friend because I wanted to focus on our relationship. However, I also asked him to stop communicating with his female coworker. He said he was willing to work on our relationship, but there weren't any definite commitments at that time.

As I made an effort to change my thinking and behavior, one thing I wanted him to do was stop helping around the house. I wanted to experience doing things on my own without his help. Partly, I hoped to develop gratitude for the assistance he had always provided in the past. I felt like I needed to do things without his help in order to learn to appreciate it. Kenny was upset by my request. He said he needed to stay busy and still wanted to take care of his family even though we were separated.

My godly aunt changed my perspective.

"It is a good desire he has for serving his family and a good use of his time."

I apologized to Kenny for trying to stop his service and focused on putting into practice what I needed to change, which was being thankful.

I found out later that during this time, Kenny's desire to help and stay busy around the house had been to stay away from temptation.

As we abstained from sex, the tension increased. An unexpected temptation for Kenny came from out of left field. Another female coworker who had not worked with him for a long time yet still had his contact information. reached out by text to offer a hookup. He told her he was married. She said she forgot, but he should let her know if he changed his mind.

After he refused to stop texting his female coworker, I still was not willing to have sex. The attraction was still there, and often, he commented on my appearance or desire for sex, which would make me angry during these times since I knew he was still not grounded in commitment.

We accepted holding and hugs from each other when we were in mutual agreement for comfort, but my sexual desire increased once Kenny started emotionally leaning toward me.

One afternoon, he was home when I arrived from work and had been helping the kids with schoolwork. We embraced, but there was passion and desire behind it. He asked if he could kiss me, and that undid our wall of resolve.

He pulled away and said if I didn't want sex, then he needed to leave because the desire was too strong. I told him I was willing to but didn't want to give it if he was going to leave me. We stayed together that night.

Unsure of what was wisest to do at this point, we scheduled another session with our counselor. Our original plan had been to work through things separately and not let sex be the tool to fix things. It had fixed things many times for us before, but it was only temporary. Sex could not create the deep change and healing that needed to occur. Only God's Word and my obedience to it would bring the change about.

Our counselor felt that if we were intimate and willing to continue working things out, it would be better to stay together rather than separate. Within that week, Kenny managed to be released from his rental contract and moved back home.

Just because he was back didn't mean we were in a healthy place or that things were easier. I felt a little more hopeful, but the work continued daily to plant good. I needed to obey God's word and put it into action in my marriage.

There was a felt lack of grace. I was afraid that if I failed again if I pushed him too much, he would walk out. It was a heavy weight to carry. I was trying to love him back to life, but the "life" he'd had just seemed to be sucked out.

He had quit his job at the hospital because of his coworker. That job was the one thing that seemed to give him purpose and joy. Now it was gone, the world was shut down because of COVID-19, and our marriage was a shell of the romantic love story we'd always idolized but never could sustain, He was filled with thoughts of failure and feelings of guilt. Depression was a heavyweight in those days for him.

When he didn't work shifts at the fire department, he would lie on the couch and watch TV all day. There was no drive or motivation. We would interact, but I always felt he couldn't connect with me emotionally.

I held many of my emotions in and found prayer and counsel from Christian friends to express my struggles. He was too fragile and unable to share my burdens.

We started going to another church, at least virtually. We also visited this church in person but with masks and spacing. Meeting people and building relationships through interaction was very challenging. I was hurting and missing face-to-face fellowship, which is why Wednesday morning video calls with my dear friend Kate, conversations with my best friend Melissa, and phone mentoring by my aunt were vital to my growth and sanity.

In late June 2020, we went on a Myrtle Beach vacation. I journaled about the lessons I was learning and the week's experiences. I still had an extreme fight with emotions. There was much I was grateful for, and overall, I had pretty good expectations for the week. However, my insecurities and grief over the lack of affection and attention from my spouse were hard to overcome.

God gave me grace, but I also used anxiety pills to manage the extreme inner turmoil. Still not sensing a spiritual or emotional sensitivity from my spouse, I felt I had no outlet that week for the grief. I didn't want to drown our vacation with wildly swaying emotions, so the pills greatly helped me to cope and focus on being together as a family and enjoying our activities.

The day I do remember breaking down was the day of our anniversary, June 28th. I slipped back to the hotel while the family was on the beach so I could write on the anniversary card I bought him. This was difficult as so much pain had occurred that year. I wrote heartfelt gratitude to have him in my life and still be together.

I was crumpled on the floor, pouring my heart into the card, trying to suppress the flood of tears and hurt.

We went out that night and walked the streets along the main strip. I got to hold a big tropical bird. We ate dinner and had a nice evening together. I was thankful that I had been able to detach enough from my emotions just to enjoy the moment.

In my journal, I wrote:

We made it to 17 years.....I still have so many questions, though, of Ken and whether my "change" will be enough to make him stay.

I want to ignore the fact his tendency to stay is only small or believe his feelings that, to some degree, he was justified by my behavior. But it doesn't help my security issues or being able to trust what he says. I know in Kenny's mind; he probably thinks he's committed and he's good. But with this having been such a stumbling block for him, I keep craving reassurance and affection from him......

Right now, I have his attention and a vacation that's paid for, and I fear his fallout. I fear being vulnerable. In my strongest moments, I tell myself I just need to give him to God and stop worrying about it. Yet my flesh rises, and I want confirmation and for him to assure me he won't leave me or pursue another woman again.

Jesus, help me walk this path with forgiveness, love, gratitude, and kindness. Jesus, be with your son (Kenny). Help him to see who you are and who he is. Ground him, Lord, and draw him to live in victory and power in You. God, help me love the man despite his weaknesses and sins. Help me to be humble with my faults and failures. I am encouraged by today's verse on the Bible App.

"So, we are not giving up. How could we! Even though on the outside it often looks like things are falling apart on us, on the inside, God is making new life, not a

day goes by without his unfolding grace. These hard times are small potatoes compared to the coming good times; the lavish celebration prepared for us. There's far more here than meets the eye. The things we see now are here today, gone tomorrow. But the things we can't see now will last forever."

2 Corinthians 4:16-18 (The Message)

Scriptures like these reminded me that though I was fighting an invisible fight with words, mindset, and actions of kindness, these things were eternal. These were the things that mattered in my life. This was the legacy I wanted to leave my kids.

I wanted to do what mattered, what made a difference, what made an impact in eternity. Choosing God's way was hard, but it was also producing fruit and a change in me that was undeniable.

Two months later I wrote another entry on August 23rd, 2020.

Sometimes, it feels like life is a big test. Some days, I feel like I'm winning, and other days, I feel like I can't tell. At least for now, when life presses hard, I am pressing back into God. I really am trying to change how

I think and react. I'm getting better at finding unhealthy patterns, but still, emotions can be hard to deal with.

I've been considerably happy the past week. I have felt good at work and good with Kenny. I've felt in love with him. We took a weekend getaway to an Air B and B retreat…..

There was an outside patio with an outdoor fireplace. We had a fire and roasted marshmallows. I asked Ken how we were. He answered he didn't know. That he felt nothing or numb emotionally. I didn't take that to mean he didn't love me, but it wasn't a comforting statement either.

I feel like I've been loving him so much. I've been vulnerable, and there are still fears I have of him being committed and honest with me. This past week, we had the whole week without the kids. We had a couple of date nights.

One night, I asked him if he knew I loved him and if he could feel it. I asked if he felt it was a role reversal (that is exactly what it feels like to me. I am now the pursuer, the giver, the open one, the romantic one.) He said he loved me but was still struggling. That he remembers how angry he was at me, he looks at the past and feels lost in the middle, not sure how to go forward. That made me cry.

He admitted I've been great, so he sees what I'm doing and how I'm acting, but to hear he still is angry sometimes or to hear him say he's lost scares me.

I can do, and be, and try to make him feel loved, but I can't make his heart change. I can't keep him faithful or committed to stay. All I can do is pray for him. If he feels lost, it shows me that he still doesn't have his grounding in God.

I feel more sane than I have probably ever been in my life. I feel more mature and seasoned than I have in my life, and I feel more control emotionally than I ever have before. But it's all because of God and anchoring those thoughts on Him and His Word. It's all about what I choose to tell myself. Fear is hard to let go of.

Right now, I want to hear words of affirmation from Kenny, but besides hearing "I love you," there aren't any other assurances….

God, I need your assurance. I need your Word to hold me and ground me in an unsteady relationship. I don't know if I can trust him, but I CAN trust YOU. Jesus, please protect my heart.

Little by little, we made progress. One of the biggest things I needed to focus on was this piece of advice from my aunt. She said,

"Focus on today. Ask God, "What does faithfulness and obedience look like today?"

It was overwhelming to deal with the emotions and the thought of plodding through the next months and years of struggles in our marriage. But often, what was overwhelming was focusing on a future that hadn't happened yet. The things I imagined were often not imagined with God's help. Yet choosing to focus on THIS day I was presently experiencing, I could walk through those challenges and focus on getting through that day, not fight the battles of days that hadn't even come yet.

In my heart, I had forgiven Kenny for his choices, but up to this point, he had not formally apologized to me for breaking boundaries and pursuing another woman. In late September, that day finally came.

September 20th, 2020

Yesterday was a good day. We went hiking as a family, and the overall atmosphere of being together was uplifting, fun, and playful....

That night, though, he was heavy with emotions. He apologized about the relationship with his coworker and leaving me. I needed to hear that as I still felt like he didn't regret or grieve over those choices.

He has had new memories pop up of the past and is grappling with that. He felt guilt over all the past sexual partners and experiences (even the childhood abuse) he had. I prayed for each person and their healing and experience with the gospel. I prayed over Kenny and his identity and faith.

God gave me grace that night, but it is hard to carry that burden. To try and be the emotionally and spiritually solid one right now. I still see him in ways, grabbing at me to save or comfort him.

God, meet him. Assure him of your presence and work. Center me, Lord. Center me on You.

My focus continued to shift, and I tried to work on more of a friendship with Kenny as well as looking at things from a team perspective. I had left so much responsibility on his shoulders for many years, looking at him more as a parent than a spouse, taking care of certain things for our family.

I was boldly stepping up to the plate and taking on things that needed to be done. I would ask for things I needed help with but tried to manage a lot on my own.

Kenny continued to struggle with depression, continued working with our counselor, and joined another Freedom Group for men. The heaviness of memories and his past mistakes weighed him down. I would feel his silence and distance and feel insecure.

When I brought this up, he explained he was battling hurtful memories. That helped me as I could understand him not wanting to burden me with the pain.

I went to my parent's house for the weekend while Kenny went to a second Freedom Conference.

One morning, I was sitting on the dock of their pond, drinking coffee and praying. My Dad came to ask about Kenny and our marriage. He mentioned that he'd heard about Taylor and her husband teaching a Bible study in their church, and he struggled with that.

"So, are you saying that because they failed, it's game over for them? If we sin and mess up, are we supposed to go around in self-abasement for the rest of our lives, never to hope we can ever be used by the Lord again?" I looked my Dad in the eye.

"King David failed big time. But that was not the end for him. God redeemed his mess, and even the line of Jesus Christ came through a relationship that was a mistake! Just because a person fails does not mean it has to be the endgame for them. Jesus Christ came to rewrite the story."

I told Dad that I hoped they would be used by God because their experience qualified them to bring something to the table that others may need. I also mentioned that Kenny's experiences could help those struggling through affair recovery.

After coming home, I asked Ken about his experience at the Freedom Conference. It had been meaningful to him. He apologized again to me for the past year for the separation and the breaking of boundaries with his coworker.

I told him about the conversation on the dock. Kenny got teary-eyed listening to the way I had answered my Dad and the way I had spoken life and faith in God to redeem and give hope to those who fail. He thanked me and was proud of me, pulling me into a hug.

I can tell you very truthfully that this is not an easy journey. But I have grown in ways I never would have, and my life is richer in spite of it. I am a work in progress, and so is my spouse. I know that no matter what the future holds, no matter the circumstances, my God will *never* leave me.

I am *loved*. I am *held*. I am a *Child of God,* and that identity can *never* be taken away from me. God promised us years ago that He was doing something new. That He would make a way when there was no way.

During the separation, another verse became my companion.

"I'll be with you. I won't give up on you; I won't leave you. Strength! Courage! You are going to lead this people to inherit the land that I promised to give their ancestors. Give it everything you have, heart and soul. Make sure you carry out The Revelation that Moses commanded you, every bit of it. Don't get off track, either left or right, so as to make sure you get where you're going. And don't for a minute let this Book of the Revelation be out of mind. Ponder and meditate on it day and night, making sure you practice everything written in it. Then you'll get where you're going. Then you'll succeed. Haven't I commanded you? Strength! Courage! Don't be timid; don't get discouraged. God, your God, is with you every step you take."

Joshua 1: 5-9 (The Message)

The promise came to fulfillment through obedience. God's word was life to them. And to take possession of the promised land and the blessings they needed to obey.

God, please make me new and continue to renew me as I walk faithfully with You. Use this story, God, for *your* glory. In the middle of a desert, *You* made a way.

Your Journey, Your Story

What does faithfulness and obedience look like today? In life lessons and trials, we will grow and be molded more like Jesus as we walk faithfully with Him.

Where are you right now spiritually? Where are you in the healing process? Mentally imagine a scale from 1 to 10. Where are you in your journey on that scale? If you identify a certain number, what is the next step? How do you get closer to Jesus or build your faith more? Is it spending more time talking to God, reading your Bible, or giving Him those fears and anxieties?

The choices we make daily, little by little, can have a great impact over time. Do your little daily decisions in thoughts, speech, and actions cultivate goodness?

If you choose to stay with your spouse, you will need to invest in the marriage. Marriage is like a garden. Thriving gardens that produce fruit take care and effort. Daily watering, cultivating, fertilizing, and pulling weeds are essential for plants to stay healthy and strong.

Marriages with good soil have a foundation where the help and healing that was needed were sought and applied. That garden will continue to grow as long as it is faithfully tended to. However, plants can die if we don't water them or withhold their life-giving nutrients.

We live in a world of instant gratification. Life is not a sprint. Run, then done. Life is a marathon. It is a journey. Finishing a marathon requires persistence and endurance. Choose to put one foot in front of the other over and over again.

We can become overwhelmed looking down the road and thinking, how can I do this in the long term? How am I going to make it through?

Here's the secret. Focus on **today.** How can I obey You *today,* Lord?

What if reconciliation is not possible for you in your marriage? The question of what faithfulness and obedience look like today still applies. Are you surrounding yourself with good people who will speak life over you? Are you seeking healing for your own life? What is God calling you to do today regardless of your situation?

Life did not go as planned, but we have a Redeemer who makes all things new. He can fill you with hope and give you the strength to move forward and begin anew.

Myrtle Beach Vacation Ken, Caleb, Todd, Allie, April

11

Embracing the Other Woman

The final chapter of my story is still to be lived, but a big piece of healing and closure occurred when I found out I would have an opportunity to see Taylor again.

I imagined it many times and played out the scenario. Sometimes, my fist hit her in the face. Sometimes, I fired angry accusations and questions of why. Sometimes, I imagined hugging her and crying but then sitting her down to talk things out. I always judged her in some way in my scenarios.

In truth, I never knew if I would ever see her in person again. Then, I found out she would indeed be coming to an event that we would be connected to in February of 2022.

Taylor. I hadn't seen her or spoken to her in six years. I mentally prepared myself. I also wrote a letter to give her, as the event didn't allow much time to talk. Our time would be short, so I wanted a way to express my feelings and the things that had hurt me.

I never got to talk to her after I found out about the affair. I found two other letters I had written her maybe several months after trying to heal my marriage. They were letters of bitterness over what I had lost because of her actions. I felt robbed in so many ways. I was robbed of friendship and trust with her, robbed of security in my marriage, and robbed of intimacy and exclusivity with my spouse. Though I never sent these letters to her, it helped me to process my feelings at the time.

No one could have predicted how I would respond to her or how that day would have gone. God is truly incredible. His timing and His ways are perfect. From the emotional level that I was at to repeated spiritual messages in sermons and life lessons, He was preparing me for that moment with her.

My letter to her this time was completely different from the others, full of bitterness and laments over lost things. Though I had mentioned loss, I also fully identified what I had NEVER lost. I had never lost WHOSE I was. My confidence and unshakable faith in my God had only increased and grounded me through that experience.

Two days before I was to see Taylor in person, a Facebook memory popped up from exactly four years earlier. This was the day I met with my friend Diana, who told me she believed I would embrace Taylor one day. That I would no longer feel like I had to compare myself with her, and that my scars would no longer be open wounds bleeding out. It amazed me that, timing-wise, these words had been spoken four years ago, and it had taken me that long to be prepared for this moment. I asked for prayer from several people who knew my situation as it neared.

One thing that helped me was choosing to forgive. I knew I had done so and would act that way toward her, but that did not mean my relationship with her would be restored or look like it had before.

The day arrived, and by God's mercy, I was surrounded by a bubble of peace and love. The anxiety, stress, anger, hatred, resentment, and pain were not present. I saw her, willingly approached her, and pulled her into a long hug. We held each other for some time. Nothing of real meaning was spoken, just polite conversation.

We exchanged letters (I chose to read hers privately after the event). At the end of the event, I hugged her again, essentially saying goodbye forever. She followed me to my car, and I asked about her children and what she was doing in her church and spiritual life. The answers were cut short by time, but I knew she could feel my love and was fully aware of the loss of my friendship and the consequences of her actions. I felt the loss, too. I miss her, in truth.

God has enabled me by grace to forgive her and let go of being her judge, but there is still wisdom in not allowing that situation to happen again and keeping a separation between our families.

I felt the freedom to love her and move on, letting go of the past and resentment to move forward with my life.

When Diana spoke those words four years earlier, I told her it was hard to believe. I couldn't imagine embracing Taylor at that time. Yet God did so much more than that. I felt an assurance of belonging to God, of being an ambassador of His love and life in a situation that otherwise was completely broken.

That is the *power* of God. *He* can rewrite stories that, humanly speaking, are not repairable in any way. *He* can do the impossible.

Every story of infidelity is different. Your spouse's or other woman's betrayal and response will differ from my story. They may never repent.

However, what happened cannot be changed. So, what will your response be? You can choose to stay angry and bitter for the rest of your life. You can choose to stand in judgment over the offenses of the other parties. But all the while, *you* are the one who is trapped. It's a heavy, miserable load to carry. It's a pain that stays with you and never leaves unless you choose to forgive and give it to God.

Forgiving them doesn't mean what happened is okay. You don't need to become best friends. But it means you can walk forward in life without constantly clenching the past in hatred, not spending hours wasted playing out the judgments you wish would be inflicted upon them. Forgiveness *frees* you.

Actions are not without consequences. The other woman feels and knows the consequences of her actions. Our friendship, in which she invested many hours, is gone and can never be recovered.

I chose to obey God by forgiving her and moving on with my life. I learn from my past, but I don't have to live there and wallow in the memory of what was or was lost.

This testimony is proof that God can help you to overcome infidelity. God can help you move forward with your life and have hope for your future.

In many ways, this was the final step I needed to process and say goodbye to Taylor.

I used to feel that I had to compete with her, and that she was always better than me. But now I know Whose I am.

I am a child of God. I have great worth. I am part of a masterpiece that God is creating. I am full of fruitfulness and purpose. God made me unique. I don't need to compete or compare myself with anyone else.

Be encouraged. This is not the end. *Your* story does not have to end here. There is a God who loves *you* unconditionally and can heal you in ways you never thought possible. Regardless of whether the relationship with your spouse is restored or not, you will be held and sustained when you trust in Jesus.

He will *never* abandon you. He is *faithful* and always will be.

I will never know what it's like to have a faithful spouse. But I know what it is to have a *Faithful God* who has never let me down. He is the Rock I cling to, the Hope I have, and the Future I look forward to.

Dear (Taylor)

I have missed you. It seems a strange way to start this letter as I also went through the whole range of emotions from being very angry at you, resentful, deeply hurt, feelings of vengeance, and feelings of deep betrayal.

Sin is a sad thing that breaks relationships and fruitfulness in life. Many times, I have wanted to vent to you my anger and hurt.

After the affair, I had composed a second letter to you at one time that I never sent. What happened, happened. It was wrong and has broken a trust that can never be recovered in our relationship. I grieve the loss of our relationship.....I grieve, never knowing what it's like to have a spouse that is faithful. However, I never lost Whose I am.

What I gained was a deeper faith in the God who has always been faithful to me. Because of Him, I will never be shaken. He is the love of my life.

Jesus is everything, Taylor. And what is awesome is that though this choice of infidelity broke many things, the story does not end there. Jesus Christ came to REWRITE that story. It's not game over, wallowing in self-pity and misery; it's moving FORWARD into what God has called you to. His words are life, healing, and the map forward into the promised land.

A few years ago, I was struggling with an area in my life that I had not surrendered to God. I came to the end of my rope, and I was desperate for change but unable to; when I cried out to Him, He gave me this Scripture promise.

"I'll be with you. I won't give up on you; I won't leave you. Strength! Courage! You are going to lead this people to inherit the land that I promised to give their ancestors. Give it everything you have, heart and soul. Make sure you carry out The Revelation that Moses commanded you, every bit of it. Don't get off track, either left or right, so as to make sure you get to where you're going. And don't for a minute let this Book of The Revelation be out of mind. Ponder and meditate on it day and night, making sure you practice everything written in it. Then you'll get where you're going; then you'll succeed. Haven't I commanded you? Strength! Courage! Don't be timid; don't get discouraged. God,

your God, is with you every step you take." Joshua 1:2-9

The way to freedom is walking with Him. It's letting those truths of the Word of God replace the lies we tell ourselves or believe. It's fully surrendering to Him and CHOOSING to obey. Once I started obeying in that area that God wanted surrendered, that's when I started experiencing freedom. That's when I started to be fruitful and succeed. He is with us every step of the way.

Obedience opens the door to blessings.

(Taylor), I pray one day, you will experience true freedom and healing. One act of obedience I have done is to forgive you. It began with a choice. I may not have felt it fully at the time, but I chose to, and that was the start.

I am free because, by God's grace, I can let go of wanting to be your judge. I can prayerfully give you back to Him, knowing that He will work out what needs to be changed in your heart and life. You are in the best hands.

My Facebook memory of the day Diana told me I would embrace Taylor one day.

References/Citations:

Chapter 1

"Here's another way to put it: You're here to be light, bringing out the God-colors in the world. God is not a secret to be kept. We're going public with this, as public as a city on a hill. If I make you light-bearers, you don't think I'm going to hide you under a bucket, do you? I'm putting you on a light stand. Now that I've put you there on a hilltop, on a light stand-shine! Keep open house; be generous with your lives. By opening up to others, you'll prompt people to open up with God, this generous Father in Heaven." Matthew 5:14-16 (Message Version) p.13

Lamentations 3:28-33 (The Message) p.20

28-30 "When life is heavy and hard to take,

 go off by yourself. Enter the silence.

Bow in prayer. Don't ask questions:

 Wait for hope to appear.

Don't run from trouble. Take it full-face.

 The "worst" is never the worst.

31-33 Why? Because the Master won't ever

walk out and fail to return.

Chapter 2

Behold, I am doing a new thing; now it springs forth, do you not perceive it? I will make a way in the wilderness and rivers in the desert." Isaiah 43:19 (English Standard Version) p.33

"See I will make you into a sharp threshing board, new, with many teeth. You will thresh mountains and pulverize them and make hills into chaff. You will winnow them and a wind will carry them away, a gale will scatter them. But you will rejoice in the Lord; you will boast in the Holy One of Israel."

Isaiah 41:15-16 (Holman Christian Standard Bible) p.42

"For jealousy arouses a husband's fury, and he will show no mercy when he takes revenge."

Proverbs 6:34 (NIV) p.44

Jeremiah 3:12 (New Living Translation) "Therefore, go and give this message to Israel. This is what the LORD says: "O Israel, my faithless people, come home to me again, for I am merciful. I will not be angry with you forever." P.45

Chapter 6

"Behold, I am doing a new thing; now it springs forth, do you not perceive it? I will make a way in the wilderness and rivers in the desert." Isaiah 43:19 (English Standard Version) p.126

Jesus said to her, "Didn't I tell you that if you believed you would see the glory of God?" John 11:40 (Holman Christian Standard Version) p.126

"Then Jacob prayed, "God of my grandfather Abraham and God of my father Isaac, hear me! You told me, Lord, to go back to my land and to my relatives, and you would make everything go well for me. I am not worth all the kindness and faithfulness that you have shown me, your servant. I crossed the Jordan with nothing but a walking stick, and now I have come back with these two groups. Save me, I pray, from my brother Esau. I am afraid—afraid that he is coming to attack us and destroy us all, even the women and children. Remember that you promised to make everything go well for me and to give me more descendants than anyone could count, as many as the grains of sand along the seashore.

Genesis 32:9-12 (GNT) p.128-129

... "he stayed behind, alone. Then a man came and wrestled with him until just before daybreak. When the man saw that he was not winning the struggle, he hit Jacob on the hip, and it was thrown out of joint. The man said, "Let me go; daylight is coming." "I won't unless you bless me," Jacob answered. "What is your name?" the man asked. "Jacob," he answered. The man said, "Your name will no longer be Jacob. You have struggled with God and with men, and you have won; so your name will be Israel." Jacob said, "Now tell me your name." But he answered, "Why do you want to know my name?" Then he blessed Jacob. Jacob said, "I have seen God face-to-face, and I am still alive"; so he named the place Peniel. The sun rose as Jacob was leaving Peniel, and he was limping because of his hip."

Genesis 32:24-31 (GNT) p.129-130

"Remember, I will be with you and protect you wherever you go, and I will bring you back to this land. I will not leave you until I have done all that I have promised you."

Genesis 28:15 (GNT) p.130

"I will make you like a threshing board,

with spikes that are new and sharp.

You will thresh mountains and destroy them;

hills will crumble into dust.

You will toss them in the air;

the wind will carry them off,

and they will be scattered by the storm.

Then you will be happy because I am your God;

you will praise me, the holy God of Israel."

Isaiah 41:15 GNT p.135-136

P.38

https://forgivenwife.com/healing-husbands-affair/

Guest post by "A Wife's Recovery From An Affair" blog

Chapter 7

Ecclesiastes 4:9-10 (New Living Translation) "Two people are better off than one, for they can help each other succeed. If one person falls, the other can reach out and help. But someone who falls alone is in real trouble." P.154

Chapter 9

"Let us not become weary in doing good, for at the proper time we will reap a harvest if we do not give up." Galatians 6:9 (NIV) p. 178

Lamentations 3:21,22-32

"I keep a grip on hope: God's loyal love couldn't have run out, His merciful love couldn't have dried up. They're created new every morning. How great your faithfulness! I'm sticking with God. He's all I've got left. When life is heavy and hard to take…Enter the silence. Bow in Prayer. Don't ask questions. Wait for Hope to appear Don't run from trouble. Take it full-face. The worst is never the worst. Why? Because the Master won't ever walk out and fail to return." P.178-179

Chapter 10

"So, we are not giving up. How could we! Even though on the outside it often looks like things are falling apart on us, on the inside, God is making new life, not a day goes by without his unfolding grace. These hard times are small potatoes compared to the coming good times; the lavish celebration prepared for us. There's far more here than meets the eye. The things we see now are here today, gone tomorrow. But the things we can't see now will last forever." 2 Corinthians 4:16-18 (The Message) p. 209-210

"I'll be with you. I won't give up on you; I won't leave you. Strength! Courage! You are going to lead this people to inherit the land that I promised to give their ancestors. Give it everything you have, heart and soul. Make sure you carry out The Revelation that Moses commanded you, every bit of it. Don't get off track, either left or right, so as to make sure you get where you're going. And don't for a minute let this Book of the Revelation be out of mind. Ponder and meditate on it day and night, making sure you practice everything written in it. Then you'll get where you're going. Then you'll succeed. Haven't I commanded you? Strength! Courage! Don't be timid; don't get discouraged. God, your God, is with you every step you take."

Joshua 1: 5-9 (The Message)

P.217-218

Chapter 11

Joshua 1: 5-9 (The Message) p.230-231